Alone Across the Atlantic

SeaBooks in this series:

Francis Chichester

ALONE
across the
ATLANTIC

Illustrated

David McKay Company, Inc.
New York

THE PRAYER OF SIR FRANCIS DRAKE
1540–1596

O LORD GOD, when thou givest to thy servants to
endeavour any great matter, grant us also to
know that it is not the beginning, but the continuing of the same until it be thoroughly finished,
which yieldeth the true glory; through him that
for the finishing of thy work laid down his life,
our Redeemer Jesus Christ. AMEN.

First American Paperback Edition, 1979

ISBN: 0-679-50901-1

10 9 8 7 6 5 4 3 2 1

MANUFACTURED IN THE UNITED STATES OF AMERICA

ACKNOWLEDGEMENTS

A solo adventure like this is in many ways exactly the opposite, it depends on the aid and co-operative effort of many people. My most grateful thanks to them:

Firstly my wife who has supported me in this project from the start and in my opinion has done as much as anyone to make the race a success. She took over the direction of my map publishing business while I was preparing for the race. She sailed over to New York while people said she was crazy to leave with no news heard of me for several weeks, and that I probably would never arrive. Finally she sailed back across the Atlantic with me.

Giles, my son, who lent me his sailing dinghy which was lashed on top of the cabin.

The *Observer* and especially Lindley Abbatt and Chris Brasher, for their interest and support in the whole enterprise, and permission to use their excellent articles and photographs.

The members of my firm including Monica Cooper, the production manager and Stuart Price, the sales manager for holding the fort successfully in the absence of my wife and me.

The Royal Western Yacht Club of England (of which Sir Winston Churchill is commodore) especially Jack Odling-Smee, Rear-Commodore, who backed this race when people said it was a crack-brained hazard and George Everitt the secretary who made the start from Plymouth such a pleasant occasion.

Robert Clark the architect of *Gipsy Moth III*, Tyrrells of Arklow who built her such a staunch seaworthy hull. David Parkes and the Agamemnon Boatyard who built Miranda. Marston Tickell whose wise counsel about storm rig, trim and tactics was so valuable.

Paddy Hare of Gowen & Co. who spared no trouble to make me the sails I wanted and which couldn't be better.

Francis Chichester

ACKNOWLEDGEMENT FOR PHOTOGRAPHS

The publishers wish to thank the following for permission to use their photographs:

1. Jack Esten. Courtesy the *Observer*.
2. Charles Hurford. Courtesy the *Motor Boat and Yachting*.
9, 10, 13b. The Author.
13a, 15, 16a. Christopher Brasher. Courtesy the *Observer*.
14. Elio Romano. Courtesy the *Daily Express*.
16b. Sheila Chichester.

BIOGRAPHICAL NOTE ON
FRANCIS CHICHESTER

Francis Chichester was born in North Devon in 1901 and emigrated to New Zealand in 1919. With Geoffrey Goodwin he formed land development, timber and aviation companies. In 1929 he returned to England and learnt to fly.

During his flying career he:

Was the second person to fly solo to Australia (1929).

Made the first E.–W. solo flight from New Zealand to Australia across the Tasman Sea.

For this flight he was awarded the Johnston Memorial Trophy for 1931. This coveted award is made by the Guild of Air Pilots and Air Navigators for the best feat of navigation during the year. The system of navigation he devised to find Lord Howe Island flying alone was the same as the standard navigation procedure adopted by Coastal Command in 1942. This flight was described in his book, *Alone Over the Tasman Sea*.

Made the world's first long-distance solo seaplane flight – New Zealand to Japan (1931).

During the first half of the 1940 war he was writing navigation instruction at the Air Ministry. For the rest of the war he was Chief Navigation Officer at the Empire Central Flying School. Here he was working on new methods of teaching low-level fighter pilot navigation.

In 1945 he started his own map publishing business – now famous for its pocket maps.

In 1960 he was on the Court of the Guild of Air Pilots and Air Navigators and a Fellow of the Institute of Navigation. Since 1954 he has taken part in 16 of the Royal Ocean Racing Club's races in *Gipsy Moth II*, during which he won the Stuart Cup for the 1956 Southsea–Harwich race.

In *Gipsy Moth III* he won the first Singlehanded Transatlantic Race, June 11th–July 21st 1960. This was also the first yacht race of any kind E. to w. across the Atlantic.

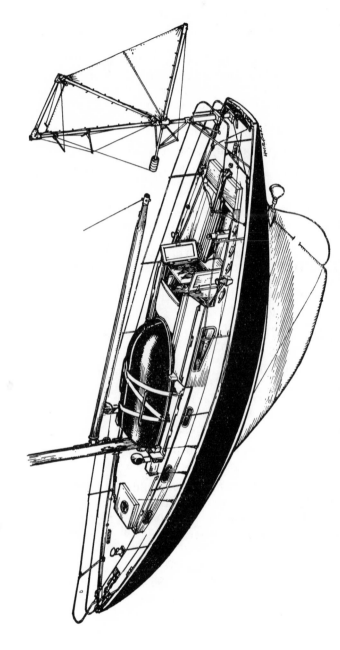

Sketch Plan of *Gipsy Moth* by Charles Hurford
(Copyright drawing the *Motor Boat and Yachting*)

CONTENTS

ILLUSTRATIONS

PROLOGUE

The idea of this race was Blondie Hasler's. Colonel H. G. Hasler is well known as the 'cockleshell hero'. As a marine commando he led some canoes up the Garonne to Bordeaux and sank several steamers in the town by fixing limpet mines to them. I think twelve marines started and only two returned.

He hoped that this race would result in getting rid of some of the chores of sailing. He thought that the competitors would more or less be forced to devise ways and means, probably novel ways and means, of simplifying their tackle and their tactics.

I saw his notice on the board of the Royal Ocean Racing Club and thought what a race of races it would be and a thrilling adventure. Unfortunately I was on my way to a hospital at the time and it looked as if my next sail would be across the Styx. However, I was one of the lucky ones and turned up again two years later to find the notice still on the board and myself fit enough to get excited about it.

I turned to and helped Blondie organize the race. It was Bill Waleran who suggested to me that the Royal Western Yacht Club of England was the right and proper club to start the race from Plymouth. We wrote to them and they were very interested. But there were a lot of difficulties. Many of the leading ocean racers accustomed to racing with full and crack crews said the solo race was a crazy hazard and many people feared a public outcry if competing yachts disappeared. They would be accused of sending the gallant sons of Old England to their watery deaths.

We were having a committee meeting at Plymouth with the Royal Western, Lindley Abbatt and Chris Brasher of the *Observer* who did so much to further the race, Blondie and myself, when it hung in the balance whether the Royal Western would take over the starting of the race. It was then that I piped up and said that if no one would organize the race, as far as Blondie and I were concerned, we would race across the Atlantic for half-a-crown. The

Americans fastened on this as a bet but not being at home with half-crowns, called it five shillings.

The race card read: Leave the Melampus buoy to starboard, (that's a buoy quite close to the starting line in Plymouth) and thence by any route to the Ambrose light vessel, New York.

Each competitor had his own theory of the best route to go. Hasler always maintained that the far north route was the quickest, that he would be in the north half of the depressions or lows up there and would have favourable east winds. Howells and Lacombe followed the low-powered steamer route, which went down near the Azores and then along the 36th parallel of latitude to end by cutting up north-west across the Gulf Stream to New York.

I carried out what we used to call in the Air Force in the war 'dry swims'. The scheme of my 'dry swim' or shall I say 'dry sail' was to take from the U.S. hydrographic chart the prevailing and other winds likely to occur in each rectangle of 5 degrees of latitude and 5 degrees of longitude and work out what would be my sailing speed for each of these winds. I then computed how long it would take to sail across that rectangle assuming I met these average winds. For example on the Great Circle route I followed, crossing the first rectangle from Start Point to 10°w. I estimated would take 62¼ hours if I had the average winds. The percentage times would be

18 hours at 2½ knots	=	45 miles
32 hours at 4 knots	=	128 miles
23 hours at 6 knots	=	138 miles
22 hours at 5½ knots	=	121 miles
5 hours calm		zero
total		432 miles
less average current		20 miles
Distance covered in 100 hours		412 miles

∴ 255 miles would take 62¼ hours

In the event with a head-on Force 6[1] or more blow I reached 10° w. on June 15th at 1600 hrs. which was 102 hours after the start. Thus do the plans of mice and men go oft astray.

[1] For Beaufort scale of wind force see p. 188.

However, I believe this did not affect the value of comparing the different routes.

The chief routes I worked over were ones actually sailed by competitors. But I tried out many variations. The old wind-jammer route, followed incidentally by nearly all yachtsmen who cross the Atlantic, went down to the Canaries and thence along the trade-wind belt to the West Indies and from there up north-west to New York. This was over 5,000 miles, 2,000 miles longer than the Great Circle route, and I ruled it out of the question for a race. I also ruled out the other wind-jammer route far north which Blondie favoured.

The Great Circle route which I adopted is the shortest possible at 3,000 miles, but it has some serious disadvantages. According to the hydrographic charts there was a 10% probability of fog over 1,600 miles of it and a mean maximum iceberg area 550 miles wide to cross. Also a head-on North Atlantic current (continuation of the Gulf Stream) averaging 0·4 knot to battle against for 2,000 miles until the favourable Labrador Current was supposed to be met at Cape Race, Newfoundland.

I consoled myself with the thought that I could heave to for twelve periods of fog of twelve hours each and still be no worse off than a competitor on the fog-free, ice-free route along the 36th parallel. Ha! what a joke, as it turned out. David Lewis in his boat *Cardinal Vertue* followed the same route that I took.

My boat is nearly 40 feet long (39′ 7″) overall with a waterline length of 28′, beam of 10′ 1¾″, draft of 6′ 5″ and Thames measurement of 13 tons. Normally I would race it in the Royal Ocean Racing Club races in British waters with a crew of six. It has berths for six. The mast is 55′ high from step to truck, the same height as my bedroom window at the top floor of my five-storied London house.

I should like to add something about the self-steering device. My Miranda is a 45-square-foot mizzen sail which weather-cocks with the wind so that the whole mast rotates. At the foot of the mast there are two arms which can be clamped tight to the mast in any position, and from each end of these arms a tiller-line leads to the tiller with

21

the result that as long as the wind vane is weather-cocking the tiller will not be disturbed.

Immediately the heading of the boat changes the wind will press on one side of the wind vane, move it, with the result that it in turn moves the tiller which moves the rudder and brings the boat back to its former heading.

I designed my wind vane myself and I based it on the model boats. In fact in the winter I studied my Atlantic Ocean racing at the Round Pond in Kensington Gardens where I went every Sunday morning for a short time and watched the model boys. I figured that if they could sail a model across the Round Pond without a helmsman I could sail my yacht across the Atlantic in the same way. My wind vane is 4½ times the area of the rudder which it has to drive.

CHAPTER ONE

April 4th to 24th

First Day Aboard – Bumps in the Night – Working in
the Rain – Rigging Jobs – First Sail Alone – *G.M.* is
Obstinate – Busy Agenda – Hard Aground – Trouble
with Anchors – The Snags in Reefing – More 'Wants'
– Blessing the Ship – on the Mud Again – Aground in
Newtown Creek – Experiment in the Solent – Compass
Adjusting – More Fun with Anchors – Disappointment
over Self-steering – Reefing much Improved – Sore
Hands

4th April 1960. We came down to Buckler's Hard on the
1st and I remained behind to go afloat on the 3rd. Usual
despair the first day at the 1,001 things to do. It seemed
hopeless and nothing worth while. It blew up in the
evening gusting to Force 6 and I hoisted the dinghy
aboard using the main halliard. I thought it would spare
me a disturbed night due to the dinghy bumping against
the side of the yacht and snatching at the painter.

I had the usual trouble getting to sleep after the first
day aboard due to over-tiredness and all the noises but
was asleep at midnight when I was woken by some
dreaded bumps which I had hoped to escape. There was
no doubt we were hitting something so I slipped some
clothes over my pyjamas and emerged in the pouring
rain and the wind. We were hitting *Gardenia* on the next
mooring. She had no mast having only been launched that
afternoon and was tide-rode[1] while *Gipsy Moth* with her
55-foot mast was wind-rode and headed in the opposite
direction. Our two sterns were hitting. *Gardenia* had a
bumpkin which I thought would be knocked off.

Now of course I regretted my dinghy was on the cabin
top instead of in the water. *Gardenia's* tiller was not locked
and hard over. I pushed it over to the other side with my

[1] See Glossary for explanation of sailing terms.

23

long boat-hook and wondered if I must launch the dinghy, a horrid thought considering the dark, the pelting rain and the gusting wind. Just what would happen one's first night afloat. One's morale and wits are at a low ebb on being woken abruptly just after getting to sleep.

My wits began to return and I shortened my mooring chain, which, with *Gardenia's* changed helm, resulted in our sterns swinging clear of each other. However I still had a bad night of bangs and bumps. Several times I went on deck but could not trace the cause. I thought it was the rain shortening the new hemp halliard. The halliard was still fast to the dinghy and I imagined the shrunk rope was lifting one end of the dinghy clear of the cabin top. No, it wasn't that. Then I thought it was a can buoy which had become entangled in the mooring chain and was bumping the yacht. In the morning I decided it must have been the mooring itself jerking or snapping in some strange way due to the shortened chain.

Today I finished stowing the gear in the cabin, filled fifteen bottles with paraffin, started and checked over the motor, bent on the mainsail. It is a big heavy sail for me. I had difficulty in topping up the boom with the mainsail furled on it, though the topping lift has a two-part tackle. I must fit a three- or four-part tackle.

Everything seems fairly in order and I hope to go off for a little sailing tomorrow.

5th April. I never got off sailing today after all. It rained off and on all day. I could hear it pattering on the deck at 7 a.m. when I woke and I felt snug and lazy and lay in the blankets till eight when I got a time signal to check the battery-driven electric clock. Every time I poked my nose out it started to rain. This happened all day. So first I did my housework, sweeping out and cleaning up. Then I rigged a tackle for the topping lift of the main boom. I rigged shock cord tiller-lines combined with cod-lines and bowsies (bowsie is the piece of wood with two holes in it as used for tent-lines. I bought a dozen from the Girl Guides head shop). As I was working hard all day it is perhaps just as well the weather was bad and I didn't try to sail. Perhaps tomorrow. Various letters about starting or finishing the SHTAR (the Single-handed Trans-Atlantic Race), obstacles, hitches, delays. I can't care any more. I am afloat, the race is on, what more could I want? Mrs. Fry says I'm mad to go in for the race. What do I care, I haven't enjoyed myself so much for years.

6th April on 'Gipsy Moth III'. Well, I finally made it — sailed *G.M.* away on my own. A great thrill. The first time is always a thriller in anything. I suppose it is because one doesn't know what will happen. I used the motor to get away from the mooring because I was not sure how much room she needed to turn. That was just one of the things we could not find out on our trip home from Ireland with the helm and rudder jammed. She turns very well under mainsail only. When tacking I would say she moves forward a boat's length after starting to turn. This may not sound much but when tacking across the river it does represent 40 feet and in places I suppose the river channel is only 200 feet wide.

It was a great boon to be able to tack up river without using a jib. That incessant sheeting in of a jib on short tacks is no joke. Of course the boat does not go as fast without a jib.

I had my arrangement of elastic cord etc. rigged for holding and adjusting the tiller but the boat seemed determined not to steer herself. At the best I could only leave the cockpit for a few minutes. I tried endless adjustments, sailing into wind, down wind and across wind. *G.M.* was not having any self-steering. She makes one think of her designer. I hope the wind vane is going to work, otherwise I shall take months to cross the Atlantic.

There were thousands of birds, gulls I think chiefly, on the spit at the Beaulieu River entrance. They made a terrific noise and I suppose were nesting there. I hove to at the E. Lepe buoy, with No. 2 jib. The boat fore-reached slowly.

How marvellous at night to see the silhouette of the woods reflected black in the still river with cloud reflections in the moonlight.

7th April. While I write this eating my lunch, I saw old *Gipsy Moth*'s scarlet mattresses go by in the fitting-out launch. *Gipsy Moth II* is lying two moorings up. It is fine and hot and I am in summer shirt-sleeves. But alas, no wind.

8.30 p.m. I don't seem to have achieved anything today and yet I have not stopped since I got up except to snatch two slabs of bread with lettuce, cheese, marmalade, tomatoes to brighten them up for lunch. The lovely sunny day ended about four o'clock and it has been unloading rain ever since.

8th April. After a good sail down river and about the Solent, when I tried out reefing, also the setting and lowering of the big genoa, I went into the Beaulieu River at only 1 hour after dead low water. There should have been 2′ 6″ + 8″ = 3′ 2″ above chart datum. I crossed the bar safely and was tacking across the river just inside when I went hard aground on the channel side of the line of stakes marking the channel edge. I dropped the main and tried the engine without avail. Then I dropped a kedge overboard. This was a mistake. I ought to have carried it out to midstream.

I was on the putty just above Rae Pitt Rivers' house. The slack of the cable enabled *G.M.* to drift downwind bumping on the mud until she reached the end of the kedge scope. In the end I ran out the main anchor with a heavy warp in the dinghy and dropped the anchor in midstream. I soon recovered the kedge but when *G.M.* floated free I could not recover the main anchor.

The wind drove the boat downstream hard on to the warp while the tide setting upstream caused the boat to lie across the direction of the anchor warp. I must have been trying for three-quarters of an hour heaving on the warp, starting and stopping the engine and trying various settings of the tiller. The trouble was that the anchor cable prevented the boat from gaining any speed with the engine on and it was impossible to steer the boat towards the anchor.

All good things come to an end, however, and when I finally got the anchor aboard I felt grateful to be strong enough to do all the heaving and hauling without having a heart attack or something and after all I had learned a very salutary lesson. The Beaulieu River is not a river to tack across at low water with 6½ feet of draught. I went aground well inside the line of stakes marking the edge of the channel. Anyway, leaving the putty episode out of it, I had a wonderful sail. What fun it is and how exciting trying out each new thing. What I learnt today includes:

(1) Under mainsail only, I can only make her steer herself by sailing close to the wind, i.e. by sacrificing speed. She will very nearly steer herself by frequent adjustment of the elastic cord tiller-lines and I hope the steering wind-vane will look after the end-piece of the control.

(2) The main halliard is very difficult to operate even with the wind no more than Force 4. I mean after reefing, when one wants to haul up the mainsail. I must fit a two-part tackle.

(3) Some sort of tackle to outhaul the leech when reefing is quite essential. I wonder if an all shock-cord tackle would work with the changing load when rolling down the main?

(4) A good thick rope tail to the jib halliard is needed, something to haul on so that one does not have to handle wire rope on the jib winch or more important, get wire rope off the winch when lowering the jib.

(5) Item, bolt on starboard half of cabin door which bangs incessantly.

(6) Item, catch on liquor locker.

I think I should add that (A) the topping lift tackle which I fitted was a great success; (B) the quick-clip hooks for jib sheets to jib clews seemed very effective and are certainly very easy to handle.

12th April. Stormy. Tacked up and down the Beaulieu River for 2½ hours in Force 6½ sometimes 7 at entrance.

The roller reefing gear worked easily and with the out-haul arrangements the sail both rolled and set excellently. Also it is not too cumbersome when one remembers the different steps. Evidence of this is that I reefed while tacking down the river in Force 6 with the channel I would say 75 yards wide. I think it would be very easy with a self-steering device but the gusts made the load on the helm vary enormously, say, by 30 lb. pull, so that I could never leave the helm for long to get on with the reefing. Of course one must expect the big variation in helm load when setting a mainsail only. A headsail would at once take most of the change of load away. Meanwhile I could not be more grateful to have a boat which will handle easily with main only. Constant fiddling with jib-sheets on such a jaunt would be too much of a good thing.

I was several times apprehensive of losing the reefing handle or the winch handle. Must think up some arrangement of lanyard whereby they will not go overboard if dropped or if they come loose.

The boat was nearly down to her lee-rail at times and a main, twice reefed as today, is nearly enough sail in such conditions. She would be better with No. 3 jib and a third reef down perhaps.

The mooring was hard for me to pick up with strong wind against strong tide. The boat really sails herself pretty fast down wind with no sail set (in such a Force 6 wind) and I ought to have allowed for this. I made about six abortive passes at the mooring from different angles and finally came down wind uptide very slowly and got the buoy aboard. I had some struggle to get the chain aboard: this is not to be wondered at considering how the yacht is now charging madly about on her mooring.

I rigged up the spinnaker boom with shock-cord at various places and hope it may keep the dinghy quiet at the end of the boom. A bumping dinghy is hell.

I arrived back wet through from neck to stern, and learnt again what a wonderful thing is whisky with lemon and hot water. Plenty is needed, however.

Must have plenty of changes of jerseys, trousers, underthings, shirts, and socks.

My line from the head of the main down about 10 feet to a suitable slide worked very well, firstly for hauling down the top of the main and then for tying it up to the mast.

A tackle or some means of finer adjustment of the tillerlines is required.

Inkoosan's owner complimented me on *G.M.'s* sailing.

28

Said he had designed *Inkoosan* himself when I asked him who had done so. A powerful-looking boat.

15th April. Watered. Filled both tanks full from empty. Took 59½ gallons. Dipped both tanks every 5 gallons and notched two dipsticks accordingly.

Could not get up to the jetty in the morning with the strong tide and against a strong wind. As soon as I slowed down, the wind bore the stem off and I lost control, risking much damage. I returned to the mooring feeling very savage at my failure. In the afternoon with wind and tide both ahead nothing could have been easier.

16th April. I was expecting Tubby (Toc H) Clayton and party. He arrived with three young men. Then Edward and Belinda Montagu came aboard.

Tubby robed in the fore cabin and held a very impressive little service of blessing the ship. There were ten of us standing in the cabin.

Afterwards the boys skedaddled in the dinghy and when Tubby imperatively required to be put ashore, I started the motor and, somewhat fortified with 'Liffey wather', motored down to the jetty. It was within an hour of low water spring tide and the mud banks looked horrible. I recalled that the harbour master had said there was plenty of depth at the jetty at any tide. However, g-dunk we were on the putty 30 yards below the jetty after turning.

We got Tubby and party off in the dinghy and he did not seem at all put out by our going on the mud. The river was emptying fast and we were well and truly sewed in no time. The H.M. came and took a warp from the masthead to the shore and pulled us over on to our side. Much to my relief because it would be no joke going over on the other side sloping down to midstream. As it was we heeled over 43° which is plenty in a boat as large as this.

We were there about three hours before refloating. When the tide came in fast we righted at the rate of about a degree a minute which was fascinating. Giles was very good with the Aldis lamp helping me up to the mooring in the dark. The Aldis beam is an unbelievable aid and joy after the torches and poor lights I have been used to before. I would say it shows objects up half a mile away.

Well, for a ship to be blessed and to be on the shore within an hour must be something of a record. Tubby told me that fishermen always insist on one net being left unblessed. Every trawler thinks he has that net and will catch fish whereas the blessing by a sky pilot will bring bad catches.

17th April. Easter Sunday. We had a delightful family sail to Cowes and then to Newtown Creek. *G.M. III* is a delight to sail and goes well. However, in the Newtown Creek I put her hard on the mud again. I was pretty depressed because it was within an hour of high water springs and with every succeeding tide lower I foresaw the yacht on her side for a fortnight. Everyone worked like a beaver and we were helped by another visiting yachtsman in a dinghy who advised us where the sand bank lay and the best chance of getting off into the channel.

We toiled away rocking the boat from side to side by everyone aboard stepping from side to side in unison. We laid out two kedges and hauled hard. Finally pulled off towards the big anchor. We had to cast off the warp to the small kedge; then the yacht drifted the other side of a perch marking the edge of the channel from where the anchor lay. The anchor warp became useless and we grounded again. One misses a reverse gear on such occasions. Our amazingly helpful friend from the yacht *Gadfly* helped free the warp from the pole and he then carried the anchor afresh out into the channel. I clapped a jigger onto the warp and set the jigger onto the cockpit winch. This has immense power and the anchor warp came aboard inch by inch until the yacht was hauled clear. The muscles in my shoulders and neck certainly ached after that little drama and everyone aboard, the two boys and Sheila, had had enough exercise. We remained on the anchor and later at dark when it was low water Giles and I recovered the kedge and its terylene warp, to my relief.

It was lovely in the creek next day with hot sunshine after a frosty night and the quiet was out of this world. We tried to land at low water to visit Dick Kindersley but could not get ashore for the mud. We had a lovely sail home. *G.M. III* seems to be rearing to go like a young horse full of oats. I believe she is as keen on this transatlantic race as I am. We dined well at the Master Builders after a gorgeous bath.

19th April. The family returned to London and I worked on board. Fitted handy stowage just inside the cabin doors for binoculars, Very pistol with red and white cartridges, Aldis lamp, torch, foghorn and loudspeaker. Rigged speedometer. Rigged compass light. After dark tried out all lights, compass, masthead, navigation. Fitted various hooks for hanging up different articles, also lengths of shock-cord with hooks and eyes for secure stowage of wine bottles and other things.

20th April. Fine sunny. Cold NNE. wind.

I went out into the Solent and tried out my reefing arrangements. The boom-end gave endless trouble and it took me 20 minutes for each set of rolls. I must get the boom-end fitting strengthened and the lugs cut off – they catch every half-roll, which is awkward unless the boom is inboard, i.e. unless the yacht is on the wind.

I also tried sailing with a genoa only. She goes much faster with the genny than with the main, 7½ compared with 5½ knots on the clock, but of course she is not so nice to tack, does not sail so close to the wind as with the main and needs the runners setting up to get rid of the sag in the luff. It was gusting and cold at times but sunny.

I lowered all sail and drifted up the Solent while I fried up potatoes, onions and eggs. The USA Vertue (*Puritan*) passed and waved; also a submarine *S 25* (but no waving).

21st April. Heard the cuckoo. Lovely spring morning, sunny. The young leaves are beginning to tint the thorn bushes. I sailed down the river, tacking in and out of the moored boats which was good fun.

Opposite the Swatch I anchored and began compass adjustment. I put down two anchors. The tide began running out like a millrace. In order to observe west on the

31

compass I anchored by the stern and stern-on to the current but she did not like it and charged about madly. I feared grounding with the falling tide but I could not regain the anchor, the current was so strong. In fact I could only move the rudder against it with an effort. I decided to anchor by the small kedge from the stem, then let go the big anchor at the stern.

G.M. has a malicious sense of humour. I laid out the small kedge with the dinghy but as soon as I tried to approach with the small kedge warp in the dinghy she fairly charged down on me like an angry bull, rode the dinghy down forcing it under the stern. I thought the dinghy and I were going to be pushed under the water. I managed to keep afloat but I had plenty of fun before I finally got the kedge laid out afresh. As soon as I had got back aboard, she became quite docile again. I shall be very wary of trying to hold her stern-on to a strong current in future; there is no joy in it.

After lunch I spent the afternoon in the yard where we mounted the vane mast to a post with only the topsail set. It worked but only just. I reckon it will need the whole sail (i.e. spanker as well) to make it effective. There is a lot to do on it but at least there is something to show. On the whole I think it will work. Will know more tomorrow when they come to inspect the fitting of the tube in the stern to hold the vane mast.

It's a grand life, how I love it.

23rd April. Today seems to have been pretty full. This morning fitting the Heron Homer D/F set which I received last night. I rigged up the various instruments in the handiest spots; the 'loop' with the compass I placed where the compass will act as a 'tell-tale' for me while at the chart table.

I left the mooring at 10.20 and sailed down the four miles of river to the bar in leisurely fashion with the light NNE. wind. The harbour master tells me there are 200 moorings in the river now.

In the Solent I first compared the speed effect of sailing dead downwind with the genoa goosewinged out on the opposite side to the mainsail and that of sailing 30, 35 or

32

L. to R.: Chichester, Hasler, Lewis, Howells (kneeling).
Lacombe arrived too late to be in this photograph.

2 *Gipsy Moth III* leaving Plymouth Sound after crossing the starting-line on June 11: the author can be seen behind the mainsail boom (*Daily Express* photo)

40° off downwind with the genny and the main both on the same side. The speed seemed unchanged. This was a disappointment because I hoped the sailing off downwind, say 30° off, would result in a higher speed which would make it worth while for the extra distance covered. I shall be unable to steer straight downwind with the self-steering vane (always assuming it is going to work otherwise) because the backstay will be in the way of it.

Another disappointment is that it is almost impossible to sail the yacht hands-off either on a reach or a run. The slightest change of wind changes the load on the rudder and if that has been trimmed successfully for one wind strength it becomes unstable immediately there is the slightest change. If the wind vane does not work I am certainly in for a gruelling trans-Atlantic passage. What I have seen so far of the makings of the wind vane does not make me happy. I think the yard have made it so heavy and cumbersome it will take a Force 3 to actuate it. (I was wrong.)

Next I tried reefing practice. With the block at the boom-end changed, the reefing was a cheering success. I took six minutes over the first set of rolls, nine minutes over the second and six minutes over the third. The sail set very well indeed; in fact I have never seen a reefed sail set so well before. So that's good. And the time taken was chiefly used in repeated visits to the helm trying to make her sail herself for a minute at a time. The changing size of the mainsail unbalanced the trim apart from anything else. I measured up the amount of sail reefed and made it 8 feet high by a mean width of 15½ feet, a total of 124 out of a total of 380 square feet of mainsail. I shook out all the reefs in eight minutes.

I scuttled back to the river using the motor to reach the bar before it became too shallow for *G.M. III*'s 6½-feet draught.

I sailed up the river till I reached a north–south reach when I picked up a mooring and began observing for compass adjustment. I took one set of readings of the steering compass, the handbearing compass and the D/F hand-held compass in the cabin, from the stern pulpit, and another set from the dinghy (as a check). All these I took while

33

headed north into the outgoing stream. I then had a snooze till the tide turned half an hour later. Then I repeated all the observations while headed south into the incoming stream.

I got lots of messages through Sheila from America and various people in England about the race, but I feel I have my hands full to get to the starting line fully prepared and I just cannot take any interest in them, or deal with them. My cabin table is thick with letters, papers, and documents about the race. Some I have not even read yet.

Got the swinging cabin table to work and left a bottle standing on it also a vase of primroses while sailing. I left the paraffin Aladdin alight while sailing and that was quite happy.

Tomorrow I hope for a full day's sailing, so that I can try running with twins. Unfortunately I have only one boom but perhaps I can make do with my very long boat-hook if the wind is light.

My hands are so sore that anything hurts them. For example I work the sink pumps with my small fingers to spare the bigger ones. My fingers so swollen that I can not close some of them and several fingernails torn into the quick. And last night I had difficulty in sleeping for longer than a few minutes because the muscle or whatever it is in my shoulder behind my neck ached so much.

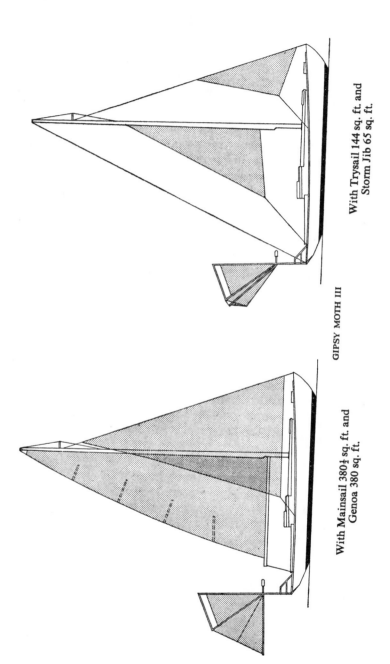

With Mainsail 380½ sq. ft. and
Genoa 380 sq. ft.

GIPSY MOTH III

With Trysail 144 sq. ft. and
Storm Jib 65 sq. ft.

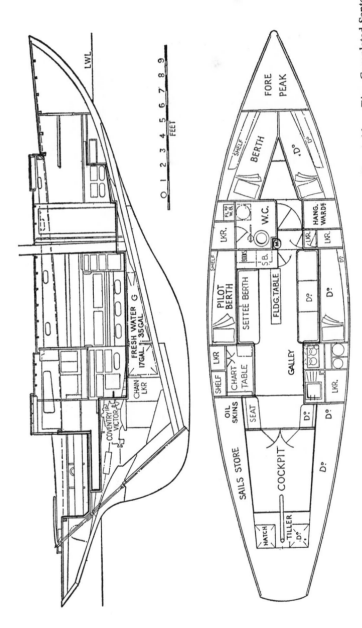

GIPSY MOTH III. Designed by Robert Clark to owner's specification 1957. Built by John Tyrrell at Arklow, Eire. Completed September 1959. Self-steering gear designed by the owner, built by Agamemnon Boatyard, Buckler's Hard.

Length: overall, 39 ft. 7 ins.; at waterline, 28 ft. Max. beam: 10 ft. 1¾ ins. Draught: 6 ft. 5 ins.

Tonnage: Thames, 13 tons; gross, 10¾ tons; net registered, 9¼ tons. Iron keel, 4¼ tons.

Mahogany planking on oak frames. Deck beams, spruce. Deck, half-inch plywood with rubber covering. Mast, main boom and spinnaker booms of hollow spruce spars.

CHAPTER TWO

April 25th to May 8th

Losing the Dinghy – Wind Vane Delays – The Dinghy
Hunt – Sunshine and Good Breeze – The Search –
Cold and Many Shifts of Wind – A Night Out – The
Thrill of the Wind Vane – Trial Run with David
Parkes – 'You Are in Business!' – Freddy, George or
Miranda? – She Works Well – Her Limitations

25-4-60.

. . . .,

Insurance Brokers.

Dear Mr Boler,

I regret to report the loss of my dinghy yesterday.
This includes a leather seat cushion, but otherwise only
the shell. It was made by W. A. Souter, Cowes, and I
will try to replace it exactly at once, subject to your
agreement.

The circumstances of the loss were: the dinghy came
adrift after snapping its tow-painter in the tide-rip outside the Bridge Buoy at the Needles. I sailed up to it
twice but there was no chance of getting hold of it in
the disturbed sea while under sail. I therefore drew off
while lowering sail, but this took a few minutes owing to
the yacht bouncing about in the tide-rip. When I
returned under motor (assuming the yacht without sail
would have much the same movement as the dinghy,
thus enabling me to get hold of it) I could not find the
dinghy. I cruised to and fro around the place for three
hours without finding it.

After abandoning the search I tried to call up Lloyds
Signal Station at the Needles with my Aldis lamp, but
could get no reply. I think another yacht coming out of

the Solent after me may have taken the dinghy while I was lowering the sail, in which case the signal station, if keeping watch, might have noticed this or might have recorded the names of any yachts passing out at the time, 1455 hours, 24th April, ¼ mile west of Bridge Buoy. You may be able to obtain information from Lloyds about this.

I suggest inserting the following ad in *Yachts and Yachting* if you agree: £5 reward for recovery of dinghy lost at Needles 1455 April 24. Thought to have been picked up by a yacht while owner lowering sail. Light blue fibreglass, white inside with red seat cushions. Painted *Gipsy Moth III* inside transom. Sculling notch in transom. Small chip at one edge of stern underwater. Made by Souter.

Yours sincerely,
Francis Chichester.

(Note to Mrs Chichester) (?)

If you have time please phone Mr Boler about this. The dinghy may be returned, it would be difficult to conceal it permanently if advertised as above, but meanwhile I urgently need a replacement.

25th April later. My letter about the dinghy loss turned out to be nonsense. When I got on to Lloyds signal station at the Needles, the man on duty told me the dinghy had been spotted near St Catherine's 252°/9½ miles at 0952 this morning. I feel the biggest clot of the south coast. If only I had kept on sailing round the dinghy in the Needles race for an hour or an hour and a half either the dinghy would have been carried out of the race into calm water where I could have handled it or else the tide would have turned and the race died down for a while.

Later the same man phoned through and left a message to ring him when he told me the dinghy had been sighted again at 1600 hours 6½ miles from the Fairway (new pillar) buoy 207° from it. I plan to get out there tomorrow and hunt for it again. It appears to be travelling NW. – SE. with the tides and I think it is worth having a shot at it – rather sport anyway. Tide turns outwards at the Needles at 1144 tomorrow. A lot depends on the wind, e.g. how fast I can get out there and where the dinghy drifts to during the night.

Long discussions with the boatyard about my wind vane. My view slightly acid as they promised it by April 1st and my trans-Atlantic passage must be a flop as far as speed is concerned if the vane is a failure. I shall need plenty of practice to learn how to use it in different conditions anyhow.

27th April. The Dinghy Hunt. I wonder when I last did as much in 24 hours.

Before beginning I slept badly. I admit I was excited at the prospect of the dinghy hunt. It seemed a highly sporting episode. I expected to be out all night and I have to admit I have not before spent a night at sea alone in a boat. And I do consider it is a much more dicey do at the mouth of the Solent than say in the Atlantic as I think my log would show.

I left the mooring late after reluctantly getting out of my bunk and phoning the Needles signal station to hear if they had any more news of the dinghy. That involved rowing down to the jetty and back; then there was breakfast with the usual household chores followed by getting the yacht ready to sail. And that in itself is something with a 13-tonner.

I motored down the four-mile stretch of river to save time in the light breeze because I wanted to reach the Needles as the tide turned at 11 o'clock. A fat chance when I didn't start till 1038. It was delightful sailing down the Solent when there was a breeze with the sun shining but I had to spoil the lovely peace by motoring every time the breeze died away. I did not want to waste any of the good visibility available for dinghy spotting. I reached the Needles at 1315, called up Lloyds station with my new toy the Aldis lamp and they flashed me 'no news'. I had trouble reading it. It is surprising how difficult it is taking in morse while tending the helm and sailing hard on the wind compared with when having nothing else to do but concentrate on the signalling.

The wind switched from north suddenly to sw. at the Needles. First I sailed south for half an hour, then west for an hour, south half an hour, east an hour, and so on, carrying out a rectangular search moving slowly southwards.

What a place England is for weather change! The clear visibility in the sunlight changed to hazy fog. Then at 1440 I lowered the big genoa threatened by a dark squall which, however, passed to the north. Then it became bitingly cold and I put on long woollen winter under-fugs, two jerseys, my kapok floatation coat and an oilskin coat on top of that. At 1700 I set the No. 2 jib and ran before the wind east for an hour without touching the tiller. I was delighted at this, the first time she had sailed herself. In my enthusiasm I put potatoes and onions to boil and opened a can of salmon for dinner but I never had it.

First the wind shifted from sw. to sse. so naturally the yacht sailing by the wind wandered off towards the north. I unrigged the boom preventer and hardened up main and jib to get on to 080°. Then the wind freshened up so I left my dining preparations to hand the jib. Hardly settled below, the wind piped up so I decided I must reef. With several Guinnesses aboard this was a slippery job and I made a mental note that I must rig up a life-line and harness. I had carried on towards the land with night coming on and it was too bad a light to spot the dinghy. A dirty rain-squall disturbed my pre-prandial peace of mind. Then at 2100 I realised we had closed quite enough with the land. I worked up a plot of the track so far sailed. I could not carry on while I ate without risk of being carried by the current into the St Catherine's race. I turned nw. but she refused to sail herself and every time I went below I had to dart back to the cockpit to set her on course again. I tipped my dinner into a jug and gave up wishing to have any.

I now wanted to settle the boat on some course so that I could sleep. I lowered the main but she began drifting in the tide towards St Cath's. Another dirty rain-squall. I tried hoisting the main partly and running nw. but it was a messy job with the sail fouling the shrouds and battens getting hooked up behind them. I didn't want a full main or I should be charging into the mainland after a few hours. Or else get much too far south if I went out into the clear of the Channel. And I did not want to waste valuable daylight returning to my search area. She flatly refused to sail north-west however hard I tried. Finally I furled the main altogether and waited to see what she would do. Round she went to ssw. and stayed there jilling along at half a knot. This was bang into the main shipping lane but I left on all the nav. lights and turned in. When I woke at five o'clock Anvil Point was blinking not far off, about 7 miles NW. One cabin oil lamp had burned out. I got her sailing north and after half an hour turned east to get to the most likely area for the dinghy. It was lovely sailing under the big genoa and full main. I fried up my potatoes and onions intended for dinner and had a hearty breakfast with two eggs and two rashers added. After sailing 8 miles east I turned north. I had to be back at midday because the yard was due to start fitting my wind vane. Not a sign of the dinghy which I had been scanning for pretty constantly while the light was good enough. Every ten minutes I scanned all round with the binoculars. At 8.35 the Needles lighthouse showed up dead ahead. It was wonderful sailing hard on the wind, bowling along at 6–6½ knots. Sun and sparkling seas, but very cold. I even dug out a thick pair of woollen ski gloves. At 1008 we were abeam of the Needles, not having altered course since 7.30. I had to tack all the way to the Beaulieu River bar but it was grand sailing. She certainly goes with such a breeze. At 1217 we were at the East Lepe buoy and at 1340 I moored on the boatyard dolphins and they began fitting the wind vane.

I needed no sleeping-pill that night. No dinghy but it was good fun and just what I needed to show what little jobs I still had to do, such as boom preventer permanently rigged, smaller block on the main halliard purchase which carried away one of the jumper struts in the dark, shock-cord preventers for the runners, life-lines, shock-cord for topping lift and various improvements to the stowage.

Let the nightingales sing in Beaulieu River; I love 'em.

7th May. Yesterday was one of the thrilling ones in my life. Cousins, the chief rigger, finished off various stays and bracing wires of the wind vane. He changed some of the slide lashings and the spanker set much flatter. Jim Crook, the engineer, cast 25 lb. of lead into three circular pieces which fitted onto an arm in front of the wind vane. These are to counterpoise the span on the other side of the vane mast. David Parkes, who now owns the Agamemnon boat-yard, came on board to sail with me. His yard had done all the work on the vane during the past two months and he wanted to see the result. He is very good company so I was delighted. We cast off.

The first excitement was when the end of one of the vane arms caught up in the tiller-line from the end of the other arm. This was while I was turning round in the river at low water using full rudder to get round in the narrow channel. The tiller-line fouling locked the rudder hard over. This was one of those moments with a moored boat now right ahead in our circular path. I called out to David to free the wire quickly and he jumped onto the counter, grasped the set-up and acted immediately. Good, that was a near one.

We set off motoring and sailing down the river, the wind being very light inland. It was obvious that the wind vane was attracting a lot of attention down the river. I'm afraid it is pretty ugly, which is a pity, but it has to be its shape to clear the backstay when it rotates.

As soon as we were across the bar I set the vane and locked it to the tiller. 'George' we called it, but it wasn't the right name. One or two readjustments and the yacht steered itself across the Solent. 'You're in business,' said David. It was a thrill; it obviously worked at least partially. We tacked up wind to and fro across the Solent. Each time I tried little changes of trim of the vane. Once or twice Freddy (George that was) took the boat across better than most helmsmen could with a straight wake not varying more than a degree or two for the 2 miles across. What fascinated me was that the topsail of the vane, about one-third of its area, was backwinded by the wind off the main-sail while the spanker, the rest of the vane sail, was belly-ing out the other way. It seemed to me that as a result of this the vane acted at once to any change of wind or change of heading of the boat. What's more the sails were quiet, asleep as the term is, whereas I had expected violent flap-ping all the time. It really was uncanny how Miranda (ob-viously female so Freddy wouldn't do) conned the boat across the sea. If set right she was more skilful than a good ocean-racing helmsman. As David said, I was in business. After all these weeks wondering if it would ever be finished and then getting faint-hearted at the thought that it might well not work anyway – and where would I be then? Certainly a very tired man by the time I reached New York. Well, here it was working better than I had hoped for. There are not many thrills to beat this one. Not only did it mean so much to the trans-Atlantic race but it was the success of a device devised wholly in a man's brain. I had imagined many, many different circumstances that it must deal with. How easy to miss out something vital, some factor that controlled everything, dominated everything. But it had come off, here it was working even better than I had hoped for.

When we had tacked up to Yarmouth (David had a two-hour zizz after the three-course lunch I cooked for him) I turned downwind and began experimenting with Miranda to see if she could control the boat while running. With the help of a jib sheeted in hard and the vane set out to leeward we ambled up the Solent with the course wandering over an arc of almost 40°. It was better than not being able to do it.

I was so exhilarated when we returned that I accepted an invitation to supper with the Garretts on their yacht *Sandera* and stayed talking and drinking whisky till 1.30 in the morning.

Today I had some alterations made at the boatyard to the clamping device of Miranda and then set forth again into the Solent with Pat and Shirley Garrett. Shirley made up a wonderful lunch with several bottles of rosé. It was terrific with salad and fried scampi.

We nearly ran down one or two boats although we had right of way in each case. Obviously some yachtsmen, perhaps not up in rule of the road, expect the other boat to give way, even if it has right of way. If that boat has no one at the helm, the result may surprise them. With Miranda doing so well, we would settle down in the cabin to lunch and time after time were astonished to find the land too close. We were charging it. It is surprising to find the Solent much too small for sailing under Miranda's control.

When we had got up to windward for two hours, I boomed out the genny with No. 2 jib set on the other forestay and ran before the wind with more than 1,000 feet of sail set. The wind was very light and we seemed to be running as fast as the wind. One could hardly expect Miranda to work in such conditions; there was no wind to move her. I shall have to rig up twin foresails boomed out and connected to the tiller, as all the trade wind trans-Atlantic crossers have done.

However, I was pleased to find the genoa boomed out well. Robert Clark had said it wouldn't and Geoff Pattinson said the boom would roll into the water. Perhaps it will, but it looked high above it today.

It was a marvellous day for England, so fine and warm. I came back with face burning and eyes aching from the glare. I can hardly keep awake.

CHAPTER THREE

May 9th to June 10th

'Racing' Against Other Yachts – Depression – The Solution – Improvements to Miranda – Happy Again – Thoughts about Fate – The Pleasures of Solitude – A Late Entry? – News of Humphrey Barton and the Trimaran from America – Chris Brasher's Impressions of David Lewis and Blondie Hasler – Sailing with Chris – Beaulieu River to Plymouth – Fog off Portland Bill – Miranda's Triumph – Last Minute Preparations and Farewells

9th May. I went off at ten o'clock yesterday and after an amusing half-hour tacking down the river, weaving among the moored boats – and it is fun because you have to gauge right each tack allowing for the slow swing round of the boat combined with the tide effect carrying it down the river – I put on the motor to get into the Solent for some more experiments with Miranda.

First of all I tried running with a boomed-out genoa but it was hopeless, Miranda needs some wind passing it to make it move whereas the yacht will run nearly as fast as the wind, with the result that there is no wind slipping past the vane, and it has no effect on the tiller. I tried lowering the main to run with genoa only, remembering Robert Clark's words to me that with headsails only his yachts naturally found their way downwind. Mine doesn't; she kept on coming up right round into wind. I felt pretty browned off. Any failure gives one a feeling of hopelessness. I lowered the genoa too and let the boat drift with the tide towards Hurst Castle while I ate a few bananas and oddments.

I thought I would get home and try out Miranda on the wind again during the process. On one tack she worked perfectly and I overhauled two big fully crewed boats also tacking to windward. Then I had to bear away, forcing Miranda round by brute force applied to the tiller, to avoid a big yacht on the starboard tack. I got a glimpse of a lot of crew in whites, her sail number was 22.[1] I tacked and went after her.

Chasing these boats, using them as trial horses, as Cutty Mason used to say, is excellent for finding out how one is getting on. In the next two tacks I lost ground badly. I could not get Miranda to do her fine helmsmanship which she had shown me she could do. On one tack we seemed to catch up but '22' began to grow small ahead. Then it dawned on me that Miranda was slipping and not only figuratively. The band which clamped the vane arms to the vane mast was slipping.

No wonder I was having so much trouble to set her. A spring temporarily inserted to make the two halves of the brake band fly apart when the clamping screw was unscrewed, was preventing the brake band from clamping tightly on the mast.

Feeling depressed was stupid because I had really done what I set out to do. First, I learned that Miranda will not work for running. I must rig up twin spinnakers controlling the rudder for that. Secondly, if the yacht controlled by Miranda could hold big, fast boats just once, as I think she did, then it is only a matter of refining her and getting to know how to handle her to do it often. Thirdly, it was good to have found weaknesses in the vane as temporarily rigged.

I felt also that David Parkes and Pullin of the Agamemnon Boatyard were right about the strength required in the vane gear. Stronger cross trees are needed, a stronger arm carrying the lead counterpoise and stays from all these arms to the top of the mast, etc., etc.

In the end we had a big pow-pow of Pullin, Haywards, Harry Cousins, and Jim Crook, the engineer, who came up in two launches this afternoon and discussed the whole vane matter. In the end they decided to add two jumper struts with diamond shrouds to stay the vane mast at the windward side, to triangulate the counterpoise arm to the two cross-tree arms and to the mast and to stay the tube

---

[1] 22 is the sail number of *Firebird X*, a 12-metre owned by J. E. Green.

on which the mast rotates with two rigid struts, one to each side of the deck forward of the vane mast.

I feel very happy again to-night. I think it will be all right. I have not enjoyed myself so much since I was preparing to fly out alone to Australia in 1929. And of course a yacht has immense advantages over an aeroplane. Here I am in the cabin waiting for my plaice fried with breadcrumbs in butter, vegetables in the thermos after being cooked first, reasonably full of good Guinness, with lovely May-leaved trees outside. It's true I wish I could have my wife here, but I do very little work when she is here, it is so amusing to talk to her. And the amount of work to be done to get ready for this jaunt is amazing.

If there is a place more beautiful than the Beaulieu River on a night like this after a fine May day, I would like to know it. The moon shines bright in the water. A wee tip of a stake sticks out in line with the twilit sky with a long V of ripples where the incoming tide strikes it. Otherwise all the trees and the stars are perfectly reflected. Meanwhile several nightingales sing at their best a hundred yards away. Occasionally there is a plop! as a fish jumps. I wonder if sea-trout are on the move.

I was thinking the old query, 'Is Fate too strong for a man's self-will?' Am I so happy because I am doing the sort of thing I was destined for? How I enjoyed – no, that's not right because I hated a lot of it or was scared stiff – my flying. No, I should say, how it satisfied me!

I'd flown through forty-eight countries, I think it was, by myself. And, apart from the flying, that represents an immense amount of preparation and expenditure of energy. At the end I said I'd had enough travelling to last a lifetime. Also – don't laugh – I'd spent on flying all the money I had saved. So I suppose I had to settle down to work. No, that's nonsense, I could surely have taken a job or something to get into an expedition going somewhere interesting like the South Pole if I had really wanted to.

Somehow I never seemed to enjoy so much doing things with other people. I know now I don't do a thing nearly as well when with someone. It makes me think I was cut out for solo jobs and any attempt to diverge from that lot only

47

makes me a half-person. It looks as if the only way to be happy is to do fully what you are destined for.

A chap came alongside today and said he wanted to ask me for various details about the race. Was it still a requirement that your boat must be painted bright yellow, he hated yellow. I learnt that he is interested to enter for the race and was considering buying *Gwynneth*, a boat in this river. I said he had better get cracking.

With four and a half weeks to go I shall have difficulty in being fully ready, though I have been preparing for months. How is he going to buy a boat now and get it ready? I looked at *Gwynneth* in Lloyds and found she was built thirty-five years ago and is only 8½ inches longer overall than at the waterline. On paper she does not sound the boat for a big ocean race against boats built for the job.

I phoned Jack Giles today. I suppose he has designed more ocean racers than anyone else bar Olin Stephens of the USA. I gather that Humphrey Barton is a pretty sure starter in *Rose of York*, a 12-tonner Channel Class boat designed by Laurent Giles. He ought to be a hot favourite. Especially as he sailed the same route in a Vertue with O'Riordan as crew in forty-seven days. He has been sailing and ocean racing all his life, could not be better qualified to win a race like this one.

Rose of York was built by John Tyrrell & Sons of Arklow, who built *Gipsy Moth III*. Humphrey offered to bring round my second spinnaker boom but Jack Giles said he had only launched *Rose of York* last week. So I wrote Jack Tyrrell and asked him to send my boom over by air or sea as soon as possible. I want to try out twin-boomed headsails before June 11th, not after.

I phoned Sheila as usual tonight and she told me that the trimaran builder from California is setting out for England tomorrow with a crew of two others. He is entering the race on June 11th. With the catamaran, we are beginning to get an interesting field.

23rd May. Arrived down yesterday afternoon after eleven days of office life. Tidied up the yacht somewhat and met Chris Brasher for dinner at the Master Builders. He had been sailing with David Lewis in *Cardinal Vertue* and with

48

Blondie Hasler in *Jester*. He was very impressed with David's boat and its self-steering. He thought Blondie's boat remarkable and was most enthusiastic about it. Empty hull. Unstayed mast. One sail which was incredibly easy to handle, reef, set, or lower. Very fast, has outsailed 'an ocean racer'. Hum, h'm.

Gipsy Moth was on the boatyard's piles where they had been working on the wind vane that same day. There was quite a lot to do to get the wind vane fully rigged, and to extricate the yacht from between two others with a fairly strong tide running. Chris had to leave at 1.30. However, with a lot of help from him we got away, down the river, across the Solent and back and upriver to my mooring on time. Chris is a natural, sailed the boat well and carried out every bit of helmsmanship and seamanship which I asked him to without fault.

Miranda took charge for a romp across the Solent full and bye, but coming back on a broad reach which turned into a dead run, she would not take control. Kept on coming up into the wind or, if I put bias on the rudder, she ran off downwind sometimes. I was disappointed. One wants more time and longer runs than across the Solent to get the hang of it. I must get out again and have some good practice. Miranda has now been stayed and braced and the clamp improved with a lever to engage the vane arm to the rotatable mast. Chris left at 1.30. He is good company and interesting about mountaineering. I think he enjoyed himself.

I started work on the yacht. One has a pretty desperate feeling on coming back. There seems an impossible amount to do and it all seems futile. This is all nonsense of course or should I say 'It is just life'. The only thing to do is to get started on one of the many jobs and then on another one, then it will seem easier and less futile after a while. If one gives way to this desolate feeling and packs up one goes back to the herd. Nothing will be achieved.

I have Sheila's photo standing up and my 'smoking' hanging in the 'hanger' compartment. It will become a home soon. Kippers and stout for tea. Bags of hard work tomorrow.

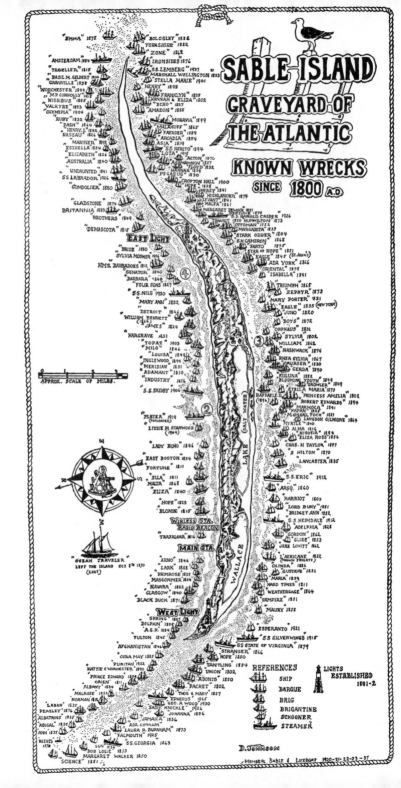

CHAPTER FOUR

June 11th to 15th

We Are Off – The Start – Wet Jumble Below –
Knocked About – Sail Changes in a Gale – *G.M.* Steers
Herself – A Spell of Sunshine – Squalls – Miranda
Saved – Treble Reefed Main – Are Trysails Any Use?
– A Fish Visitor – Going South? – News of Blondie
and David – Slow Progress in Summery Conditions –
Water Everywhere – Biscuits or Medicaments – Toe
Trouble – Dirty Morning – Struggling with Sails –
Headwind Again – Tilley on Stern – Electricity Gone
– Ostriches or Emus? – Dining with Difficulties

11th June. 1109 hrs. Enjoying a whisky and lime plus biscuits after strenuous start. No particular blacks. Must have
had race fever because I could not eat any breakfast, but
had two Sea-legs (anti-seasick pills) instead. Will probably
shake out reef after refreshment. Feel better already.
Stowed Plymouth charts.

I only cursed one boat for baulking me at the starting-
line, my friend the ex-King's Harbour Master whom I sat
next to at dinner. He was baulking me just before the
starting-gun and I said, 'I wish you'd get to hell out of it.'
Of course I wish now I hadn't said it. The Navy moved
away one trawler loaded with sightseers. It is something to
have to dodge launches, one's rivals, etc. as well as get
across a starting-line single-handed.

Things went fairly well but of course it takes me longer
to set sail and the small boats got away ahead of me.
Blondie's boat looked quaint. I saluted them all. David
tacked inshore after the breakwater. He was well to windward of me then and not far behind. My hat! that whisky
was good. . . . I must have another! 1545. I streamed the
log 40 miles after the start.

1738 hrs. Much to my disgust find I should tack as the

port tack is nearer the Great Circle course of 275°. Feel awful, but had a cup of tea and a few cream crackers.

12th June. 1630 hrs. Written over a cup of tea in a bag which you hang in the cup and pour water on. I wish I could light the Aladdin oil stove. Well, why not? Hold on while I try. . . . It seems to be working all right.

Everything that isn't wet is damp and clammy. My lovely boat. What a mess! My wet clothes piled on the floor. Stuff jumbled everywhere. Bang! occasional waves hit the hull so that you think it's the *Queen Mary*. It is impossible to stand up anywhere without using a hand-hold. Anyway I feel better. Seasickness stopped and not faced with any horrible manœuvre at present.

If anyone is short of exercise I can recommend furling a 385-square-foot mainsail of heavy Terylene in a gale. No, it's not too bad but by the time the other jobs demanded by a gale have been finished you feel you've had a run-around. First, lowering the mainboom to the deck and lashing it. Then setting the trysail with a four-part tackle to bowse it down and two three-part tackles for sheets all with heavy double blocks. Then there's the wind-vane spanker to hand which involves some nice finger-work while the vane dashes too and fro with the changing blasts of the wind. Then, set a storm jib – fairly simple by comparison.

At last the boat is sailing along fairly satisfactorily even if damned slowly with trysail and No. 3 jib. She gets a bit temperamental now and then when two or three big seas hit her one after the other and she then tacks herself. Twice I got out of the bunk, put on big boots, oilskin trousers and coat, hat and towel round neck to get her back on course. The second time I found to my astonishment, arriving late, that she had sailed herself right round in a circle and come back on course again. So next time I stayed in my berth and watched this amusing antic reflected in the tell-tale compass.

I propose keeping on this course estimated at 225° (sw.) with the storm rig set until this little storm blows itself out.

I can do with an easy time tonight. Apart from fatigue my chest is fairly sore. After bashing the right breast when the door of the heads burst open and I shot across the companionway, I was in the cockpit steadying myself against the hatch when it slipped forward a foot and the top corner of the cabin door stabbed me in the left breast. Never a dull moment!

13th June. 0220 hrs. Woke reluctantly and dressed in full kit. 2 a.m. Hell of a night on deck. Force 8/9 gale. Driving rain. Lumpy seas bashing the hull. But the crew seemed quite happy. Miranda unfettered, i.e. out of use. Tilley shining a lovely white light on the sails (I repumped her) but she is dimming. I guess her bottle refill is ending. Only old Log unhappy, tied up in knots and only registering 3½ miles from 2320 to 0220 hrs. Whereas I should say we are doing 6 knots at present.

Thank heaven and Marston Tickell (who made me take it) for the trysail with its powerful treble-part tackles, port and starboard, to the clew of the sail! *G.M.* seems to be self-steering well enough with this rig, course about 220°–260° but she did a complete 360° turn while I was on deck so I hardened the weather tiller-line slightly. It may mean a few degrees' worse course, but worth it if it prevents the shattering flapping of the trysail when she tacks herself.

Will have a cup of hot water in thermos with some sugar in it. Took two Sea-legs at 2330 but still queasy. No food except a few biscuits, etc. since the day before the start, i.e. three days ago.

2240 hrs. Seems much quieter on deck now; it must have been a squall. I would have been badly placed if I had had normal canvas set.

I have found that by stripping down the upper part of my oilskin – pvc really – trousers over the long sea-boots (calf high, I mean) I can take off the boots and trousers together and put them on together next time. Trying to draw oilskin trousers over boots or under boots in a yacht in a gale is no joke.

0255 hrs. Poked my nose out: it is still pretty foul weather. Thank heavens for my crew carrying on while the skipper takes to his berth. I not only have the cabin doors closed tight but have stuffed an old copy of the *Daily Express* into the ventilation opening to keep down the inrush of clean, untainted air, Force 8, into the cabin.

0830 hrs. Monday morning . . . and the sun shining . . . I'm drinking tea after waking and life seems it might be good. I could have done with even more sleep. I woke once about 5.0 and thought I ought to crack on more sail but thank heavens there was the father and mother of a squall — wang! bonck! What a lovely lullaby, seas crashing against the hull. Spluuuunnnchch! as the bow seems to drop into a trough. I estimated it took thirty seconds after a sea had broken on deck before the water finished running out of the lee scuppers. Anyway it was good enough for me to turn over and sleep on.

I'd like to have gone on sleeping now but I thought of that damn black-bearded Viking cracking on sail. No fatigue trouble for him! He may have a smaller boat, but be sure he is sailing it at its maximum speed every minute. What a grand chap.

I'm stiff and sore and tired. Both sides of my chest hurt from the blows I had. I cut my scalp on the ceiling (my own fault). I really ought to try one of David Lewis's concoctions on it, some dehydrated ointment I should think. I had an insult of an injury too. The heads door slammed and caught the pelt over my ribs in a damn painful pinch. What an indignity to be caught by the skin in a doorway!

Hullo . . . she's tacked herself and is boxing the compass again. You may wonder why I sit here writing. One, I'm sipping tea and infusing a bit of joy to the system. Two, I'm listening and assessing what sail I can set. It's no joke to make a mistake in this sea — it's a laborious job for me to change sails.

As I write we are going into a black-clouded squall so it's a good job I was not in too much of a hurry, Blackbeard or no Blackbeard.

As you may guess my sea-sickness has gone, thank heaven, and I can think of serious toil. My last meal was that fine farewell dinner at Pedro's in Plymouth on Friday night. With the sunshine I feel the weather must be on the point of improving fast, squall or not.

1050 hrs. I still have not changed up any sails and another squall is on us now. I have reset Miranda and been

54

watching her performance. I have too little sail up but the squalls are very tricky. Will have a meal and think again. Softlee softlee catchee monkey, I say.

At 0030 hrs. I was woken up by the boat tacking herself with Miranda set, topsail and spanker. I rushed on deck but not in time to counter the tack. However, I topped up Miranda so that she would not be smashed against the backstay if she sailed round in a circle. I'm not satisfied about her conduct, naughty girl. I then set to and lowered the trysail. Then hoisted the – Crikey! The whole ocean seemed to dump on top of the boat; I jumped in my seat, but marvellous! none below – well, I hoisted the main triple reefed. The boat began to sail.

I'm not sure my old theory about a trysail isn't right. Better to set no sail till you can hoist the main again. Trysail speed is so slow and it takes so much out of the crew to hoist and lower. It took me an hour and a half to do those two jobs, trysail and main and damned hard work hanging on like a monkey the whole time.

I found a fish washed on board. True it was only a baby sardine but still a fish. Then I studied Miranda. The handle which clamps the vane mast to the vane arms which pull the tiller from side to side was being unclamped when it came up against the backstay. I hacksawed off a piece. Then I found the clamp was slipping, which may have accounted for M's lapses from good behaviour.

This was a difficult job on the counter with the stern dancing every way and swishes of water coming over the stern deck from waves hitting the foredeck. Although it only involved removing a spring and washer and sawing off part of a bolt it was awkward and took time. I felt that depressing despair that we all get; but the job was done at last with no vital parts washed overboard.

My best course for New York is 288° magnetic so the course we are on at present of 240° is as good as the other tack. I never meant to go south but perhaps it is fate. That sardine and the sun make me think of flying fish for breakfast compared with possibly 1,600 miles of fog on the Great Circle route to Cape Race. I should think that black-bearded Viking must be ahead of me at present. He can change his sails in a twink and has no fatigue problems.

I heard on the BBC when listening for a time signal and weather forecast that Blondie has passed the Lizard yesterday afternoon. (My word! Some whacking big seas hit the hull at times.) I reckon I was about 45 miles sw. of it at one o'clock yesterday afternoon. David, the BBC said, had lost his mast and returned to Plymouth for repairs before setting out again.

14th June. 1310 hrs. This is very pleasant; the sun trying to push through a layer of summer white cumulus high up; south breeze; but as for racing weather.... To start with, the breeze, like all the wind we have had so far, is from New York, so, with gale or light air and Miranda in charge, we cannot point within 55° of New York.

So far it's the slowest race I can remember off-hand. At 1130 this morning I was only 186 miles sw. of Plymouth after three days. Can I believe it? It seems incredible.

At 0900 hrs. (I didn't get to sleep till 4 a.m.) when I woke, I found the yacht headed 340°–350° compass so decided the sw. tack better. So I tacked to starboard tack again but first set the big genoa in place of the 225-square-foot No. 2 jib. The genny is 380 square feet. Then I had breakfast of toast with some of Mrs Philip Yonge's scrumptious home-made Devonshire butter, grapefruit and coffee.

Then I found the sw. course had dropped to 210° compass so decided the north-west tack better and tacked again to 325° compass. But now, later she is only sailing 335° compass which is just as bad as it could be, i.e. the wind is dead on the nose for New York and only a light breeze. I shall not be there till autumn at this rate. It would take about sixty days anyway.

I surveyed the boat.... It does seem incredible to me: I reckoned this was a watertight boat without a leak other than (1) one place over the port side pilot berth which I and the boatyard have both tried to cure; (2) a weep at one corner of the forehatch over my berth in the fore cabin; (3) a good deal of leak from the foreward end of the cockpit onto the bridge deck below. I cured a lot of that one with a patent seam-sealer which is squeezed out of a tube like toothpaste. Other than that the yacht was bone dry and I had pumped no water out of her in three months afloat.

But when I look round this morning, the whole cabin sole in forecabin, main cabin and heads looks as if it had been out in a shower of rain. Every wall that I can see is dotted completely with water drops as if caught out in a quick shower of rain. They show clearly an angle of heel, i.e. slope. It appears that every wall in the boat is streaked. Where did it come from? I can see where a good deal came through the ventilators and where the mast passes through the cabin roof but I can not understand how each wall is streaked or spotted all over. I can only think that the tremendous weight of heavy seas bursting on deck temporarily opened timber seams and shot through a shower of spray.

The noise the seas made was terrific. So much that I several times started getting out of my berth thinking the yacht had been struck by a steamer or that the mast had gone overboard. One sea last night when I was asleep not only jumped me up in the air from my berth but lifted the heavy tight-fitting wooden settee on which I was sleeping and dumped it out of place so that I had to get out and put it back again. But sailors don't care, they say.

What a marvellous feeling when you find the boat is sailing on regardless. I reckon she is damn solidly built. Good luck to Jack Tyrrell of Arklow in Eire, who built her. But by heavens I wish he had kept the leprechauns out of of the locker fittings. Half the doors and lockers spring open when things are hectic.

All the same, I wouldn't swap places with any person in the world at present. I am only disappointed in the delay for I admit I greatly hoped to make a fast trip which would be hard to beat. However, I'm still in the race.

I wonder how such hard weather affected the other chaps. Undoubtedly I must lose a lot of time by taking longer over sail changes so that frequent changes of wind and weather favour them. I can't see them doing much less worse, better if you like, than me in heavy weather. If it was hard for me to make any headway against those seas and wind it must surely be worse for 5-tonners. I think they will gain now that it is a light breeze.

I believe that black-bearded Viking will sail faster than I in light airs. He has a lot of sail for his folkboat and I expect also that his boat would point closer to the wind than *G.M. III.* What I need is a steady reaching wind of Force 5 for a fortnight. I ought to have an advantage then. Other than that the Viking will gain in several ways. No effort for him to change sails or tack and without delay too while I lie asleep. I ought to have named this vessel Gipsy Tortoise instead of Moth.

The picture which Tubby Clayton (Toc H) gave me after his service of blessing of the boat on board, a reproduction of an original lithograph of the Tower of London and the Mint still stands apparently undamaged though backed up to a wet-speckled cabin wall. (Tubby would have made a wonderful map and guide publisher . . . his knowledge of London is amazing and fascinating.)

My framed picture of Sheila did not fare so well. Water penetrated the frame and – because of the salt, I suppose – played havoc with the photograph itself as if it continued to develop the print. I am sorry because it is a lovely portrait of her when we were married, photographed by Lenare; I fear it is not replaceable.

15th June. 0430 GMT . . . I'm staying in my berth awhile to see if what might be a black squall ahead is or not. It was still dark night when I got up just now and went out for my two-hourly inspection. I had expected to find it light enough to turn out the Tilley lamp in the stern but I had forgotten that, with the longitude west increasing, dawn is later every day by four minutes per degree of longitude. Assuming of course one sticks to Greenwich Mean Time on one's clock – and watches.

There is something pretty awe-inspiring if you go up on deck at night when there is a bright light in the stern. At first it seems that black Hades is rushing past. Then one's eyes get accustomed and one begins to see there is a sky after all. Now, with dawn lightening the sky astern, it begins to look more friendly.

I wanted some biscuits while waiting and sipping a cup of tea from the thermos. I know the boat is stuffed with biscuits but could I find a packet without unpacking a deep drop-locker behind the stove (not a job to be done lightly). Everywhere I looked I seemed to be baulked by

David's niceties – dehydrated antibiotics for fiery appendices for example or shark repellent.

Damn! I put my dry trousers in what I thought was a dry place and it turns out to be wet. The only thing to do if you have some dry clothes is to wear them while asleep. Well, here is the squall; I must go on deck.

0600 hrs. It was short but sharp. I had to get the genoa off. I lowered it flapping madly, dragged it out of the water bit by bit (at least it was quiet in the water) and lashed it to the weather life rail.

It is calm now but I think there is another squall ahead, so I have not set any foresail. I'm hoping I can leave the main unreefed because I don't want to use up any more energy than I have to.

I went out barefoot and found it a success. I stubbed my toe really hard when hauling on the main halliard. It was so painful that I could not bear a shoe on it. I had great trouble yesterday afternoon keeping my balance. I thought at first it was the Guinness I had for lunch but later decided it was the damaged toe. Just now without anything on it to hurt it I had no trouble about balance. The question now is, shall I change into dry things or remain on call in my wet ones. I think I'll go out again now, reef the main and then turn in for some more sleep.

0730. In the end there was another squall and I lowered the main in a hurry to avoid damage. Then I decided to call it a morning, furled the main, topped up the vane spanker and handed the log.

We are rolling like I don't know what. There is a breeze between squalls but I intend to have a sleep first. Plenty more squalls ahead by the look of it.

1340. The barometer is still high at 30 inches so perhaps it is only a trough of low pressure going through. In a way I couldn't bear to set fair weather sails again today.

I've seldom had a fuller morning. After an hour's sleep I got out of the blankets at 0900, looked at the weather and got back again. A dirty morning, plenty of wind, a lumpy sea, cloud nearly on the deck, nasty dark storm stuff around. Much better wait a few hours in the hope of its changing and save my strength. However, after a few minutes I got out and dressed in my wet clothes. Nothing cheers up a man less than getting into sodden clothes. But the yacht is smothered in wet things already so I wasn't going to wet another set.

Everything takes so long in bad weather, dressing for example when unable to stand without using one hand to hold on with. What a morning! I didn't finish till 1230 – 3 hours to set sail and the rest. It took me 1½ hours to hoist the main and reef it. This sounds absurd I suppose, but one item alone is to get the 18-foot main boom topped up off the deck without busting gear or being knocked out.

I had to balance on the counter aft of the boom-end swinging to and fro and slack off the main sheet with one hand while I hauled on the topping lift with the other – Oh! for the strength of that black-bearded giant! – then, as I couldn't turn into wind to hoist the main, the slides jammed in the track and the sail with its battens fouled the lee shroud and runner.

During all this picnic the boat is rolling like, well, you know what, and bucking, rain falling in plenty with periodic sluices of sea. One can feel desperate with all the to-do but I doled out good advice to myself: Don't hurry! Take it slowly! You are bound to get it done sooner or later.

I consoled myself with the thought of what a ridiculous figure I must look barefooted, Jaeger's long woollen scarlet underfugs down to my ankles, black oilskin down to my knees and a dark-blue deerstalker down to my chin.

I nearly got the main up when the flogging of the sail against the shroud started a 3-foot batten from its sheath. I hurriedly lowered the sail and managed to grab the batten, now half out of its pocket, before it flew off into the sea. Bit of luck; I have lost one already.

When I got the main up I wanted to call it a day; but the boat was hardly moving. I think the rudder has to be so hard over when there is no foresail that it acts as a brake and stops the boat. Finally I decided there was nothing for it but to set a jib and I plumped for No. 3 jib which is about 135 square feet. I got out a pair of wire sheets and rove them carefully. Then I cleared the jib-halliard which had got behind the cross-tree.

Finally I hoisted the jib. The boat sprang forward at once and began charging through the seas, bashing through. It

60

was quite thrilling and I got a good satisfaction at having stuck at it.

Of course, the jib sheet was in the wrong place, on the wrong side of a life-line, and I had to bring round the other sheet from the weather side and hold the jib on a cleat while I changed the wrongly aligned sheet. Then I bagged up the genoa full of salt water.

Meanwhile the signal halliard had been broken by the runner flying round but it had got fouled after parting and I had the luck to catch the end before it disappeared aloft. After fixing that, I noticed that a shackle on the topping lift had failed or unshackled itself. Again I was lucky enough to catch the flying block of the topping lift before it went aloft where I pictured it twined round a cross-tree. It was a bit dicey, as I had to balance on top of a winch in order to reach the flying block but I had on a life-line.

After all this fun and games I thoroughly enjoyed my breakfast at 1315 hrs. Now at 1420 hrs. the weather looks like improving and the wind is dropping. What a life! It will just have to keep dropping for an hour or two while I have a quick zizz and work out a position from radio beacons. At least we are headed right, 290° on the compass. I must just pop out and see how the log reads since setting the jib.

11½ miles in 1 hr. 55 min. = exactly 6 knots. Amazing how she sprang forward charging through the waves as soon as I hoisted the little jib.

1530 hrs. Wind veering, headed us to 330° – Marston Tickell would be pleased. I have somewhere on board his essay on 'It pays to be headed'. Amazing what fine racing sailors the Royal Engineers make.

I stirred myself and emerged. Tried to get on a boot to keep dry but my blackened toe would not stand it. Nearly midsummer and I am wearing thick woollen underpants (long edition), track pants of woolly stuff (right shape these for boating), Viyella shirt, sleeveless jersey (knitted by Sheila years ago) plus a thick woollen sweater.

I hardened up the sheets of jib and main and retrimmed Miranda. New course 310°. Thank heaven, enough wind still to justify not shaking out the reef or setting a larger headsail.

Now for a cup-of and position-fixing by radio beacons. Still making 6 knots by the way. It's odd that a full cup of tea can sit on the swinging table whereas I can't hold one without spilling it. The table is beaten, however, when the yacht pig-jumps and the cup jumps up. It looks to me as if a yacht ought to have a swinging seat combined with the table; one could then pursue one's knitting urbanely regardless of the effects of the elements.

1600 hrs. Position by radio beacons and dead reckoning 48° 10′ N. 10° W. Best course for New York . . . 291° compass. It is rather a poor showing that we are only 270 miles on our way in a straight line from Plymouth in 4¼ days, an average of 2·7 knots or only 65 miles a day. But what miles of physical jerks included!

The beacons I used for the fix were Cabo Vilano in Spain, Ushant in France and Round Island, Scilly Isles. Would like to have used Mizen Head in S. Eire but Vilano was signalling at the same time and drowned Mizen Head. Another day should put me near the limit of the radio beacons and I shall have to trundle out the old sextant.

I want three days dry, sunny weather. I should say half the contents of the whole yacht need taking out and drying. For instance I found the little sail of Giles's sailing dinghy which I am carrying on deck (I mean the dinghy; the sail was in the sail stowage) was running with water. However it is no good worrying about that at present.

Blast! the wind is moderating. I shall have to turn out again and set a bigger jib, I suppose. The weather looks horrible still. Dull misty murk all round with low cloud or mist nearly on the sea. The sea is moderating too, though a crasher landed on top of the cabin a few minutes ago. Probably only a couple of bucketfuls but it sounded very impressive.

I wonder how my rivals have fared. None of them could lose all the time it costs me to handle my big sails but if I can't stand up in this 13-tonner without holding on what must it be like in a 5-ton folkboat? If they don't get seasick with the twisting and dancing, they must have the internal layout and spleen of a boa-constrictor. The idea of a black-bearded boa-constrictor is quite a novelty.

Midnight. Chagrin. The Tilley lamp went out in the

stern. I switched on the masthead light, no response, then the navigation sidelights, no response. I found the new port and starboard lights fuse had gone as did a new one I put in. A new fuse for the masthead light made no difference so I suppose the bulb has gone. No lights.

It's a queer feeling charging through the night in bad visibility. The mist, almost fog, if not in fact fog, only gives a few hundred yards' poor visibility. With that bright light shining it is not so bad. I lit the Tilley again and now keep watch like an anxious hen fussing over its chick.

At 1830 hrs. I could see I was losing a lot of speed by not carrying more sail. I set to work at once and though I consider I know the drill fairly well it took me 1¾ hours: chiefly to change the No. 3 jib for the big genoa. I had a lot of sheeting hold-ups. Usually that's the trouble with complicated settings, I had been using the genoa block for the No. 3 wire sheet. By trying to introduce a new block, which was an inch or two higher above the sheeting rail I got an overrun on the winch. An incoming turn overrode the previous turn on the winch drum. With a powerful sail like that genoa this is a serious labour. Maybe the easiest way of dealing with it in the long run is to lower the sail and start afresh.

After trying one or two ideas which all failed I succeeded with a very simple one, I fastened another rope to the iron-bar tight sheet and took the strain on the mainsail winch. I think the naval term is 'clapping a jigger on to a cable'. I only mention this to explain where the time went.

As I took the proper strain on the genoa sheet an extraordinary phenomenon occurred. The yacht went quiet and was off. I felt she smiled to herself and said, 'This is what I've been waiting for.' She has a queer movement, a sort of quivering undulating or wobbling as if she were shaking her powerful haunches in a wild silent gallop. No, not gallop, running stride perhaps like an ostrich. I say ostrich though I have only seen cassowaries and emus running really fast with me behind them in my aeroplane. I wish I could describe this movement. No fuss, no disturbed wake no noise but still it was hard to stand up.

For two hours she did 8¼ knots and is still averaging 7½. This with a double reefed main. It seems pretty eerie on a dark foggy night. I've given up shoes and boots and I'm grateful that my port settee berth and the pilot berth alongside are both dry. I did not have to dip the gash bucket in the sea for salt water. I dipped it out of the self-draining cockpit. Dinner was difficult – once I pitched into the galley stove and knocked it off its swinging frame – but I had a meal nevertheless.

CHAPTER FIVE

June 16th to 18th

The Sick Tilley – Miranda's Slip – Ideal Sailing –
Steamer in the Fog – Calm after Rough Night – Call-
ing without Reply – Hove to – Loss of Racing Flag –
The Twins for the First Time – About Washing up
– Talking to Oneself – *Gipsy Moth*'s First Real Run
in Her Life – Favourable Breeze – The Moth

16th June. 0145 hrs. Tilley went out again at a quarter to
one. Blew back this time for a change. Seems a bit off-
colour tonight. I wish David had given me a potion for a
sick Tilley. I lit her up again but also fished out the copper
riding light which has never been lit. I have turned it up
and it now sits on the table in front of me. Maybe Tilley
didn't know she had an understudy waiting for a chance to
take over. Perhaps she will try harder now.

We are still on our way at 7¾ knots. I would say we are
within 10° of hard on the wind. Perhaps Miranda is respon-
sible. She went quiet too as soon as I set that genoa, not a
flutter – just a gentle weaving movement like a fish keeping
station in a stream. Whereas, before, in the bit of a blow
she was flapping and snapping, and jigging about and we
were all getting almost nowhere very slowly. I think I shall
turn in for a couple of hours till dawn. Dawn last night
about 0415 so it won't be till about 0430 tonight, farther
west.

0920 hrs. I woke near eight o'clock with a start. On the
point of springing to the tiller; the yacht had tacked herself. I felt her come upright and then head the other way.
Automatically I looked at the pendulum measuring the
angle of heel – as I was getting out of the blanket – and
was astonished to find the boat was still heeled 25° to starboard. She had merely eased up suddenly from 45° This
illustrates how completely one's senses can be fooled – as,

of course, one knows well from blind flying where one can't even tell if upside down provided that gravity is first counterpoised by centrifugal acceleration.

Forgive my prosiness. I want more sleep. I can't relax when charging through a dark foggy night even if not in a shipping lane. Next my tell-tale compass – what a pal! – told me we were headed up to 350° and once up to north and I girded up my mental loins to spring, however lethargically and reluctantly, to the tiller and change tacks. Then I thought 'Hold hard a minute. The thinking box is befudged, have a cup of coffee first. Anyway, it may save a blunder in handling the gear.'

So I coffee'd and then read the log and looked at Miranda's set-up. Firstly she had slipped a little. The incessant jerking had slacked up a bowsie on a tiller-line. It is amazing how those things hold at all. I think I explained that they are only bits of wood with two small holes to take the tiller-line and are meant for taking up the slack in tent-lines. I bought them from the girl guides' shop. I adjusted the lines and found she would steer 310° at a slower speed.

Then I worked up the dead reckoning from 1600 hrs. yesterday and found that at the present position 49° N. 12° W. after allowing for magnetic variation and compass deviation, she can still stay on this tack on the present heading within 19° of the best course for New York.

We sailed last night 86 miles in 12 hours 15 minutes – just over 7 knots average. Wonderful sailing! This is what I came for. But how seldom does one get it especially on the wind. Now the wind is a good deal easier and I must shake out the reefs and retrim. Out damned lethargy!

Bong! *Gipsy M* has learnt how to unseat a cup of tea at last. She pig-jumps to port and while the swinging table is still swinging she pig-jumps to starboard. It's an old bronco trick for throwing a rider, changing direction of a buck while still in the air. Mind you, she waits till I have a spoon in the cup which just does the trick for her. I think she is annoyed because I ticked-off Miranda. She tried the same trick again while I was mopping up the coffee and pitched an open, nearly full, pot of runny honey into my berth among the blankets. But I was too smart for her and though it fell on its side I fielded it before a drop of honey passed the edge.

During the night I suddenly realized what the movement was like which I was trying to describe, a fast horse going over rough ground strewn with fallen timber. Anyone who has ridden a lot will know what I mean, the rising upthrust like the beginning of a buck as the horse flies the log and the wobbly quivery swerve as she avoids something.

Avaunt the prattle! To toil! To toil! To toil!

1055 hrs. I figure someone on this boat has a sense of humour and not of the best kind either. When I went below after finishing the unreefing of the main, the riding-light was lying, resting you might say, right in the middle of the blankets on my berth. The lamp must now be pretty well empty of paraffin, which has soaked my blankets. Why I mentioned sense of humour is that it was exactly on the spot where the pot of liquid honey landed a short while before and which I fielded before the honey flowed out. I must have some garlic for lunch to counter the smell of paraffin.

1600 hrs. Fog. Not thick but still fog and reducing the visibility to say a quarter-mile. My route goes through an area of 10% probability of fog, drawn from thousands of observations, which is 1,600 miles wide from E. to W. and 40% probability for an area several hundred miles wide centred on the Grand Banks south-east of Newfoundland. But that area does not start for 1,000 miles west of here. Of course there is always a chance of fog anywhere. I hate the stuff though I must admit I've had quite a lot of exciting adventures due to it while flying.

This afternoon after a sleep I achieved a shave. It wasn't very good; there are several patches unharvested. One needs to be a balancing acrobat to shave, although the boat now seems quiet. One trouble was to keep the water in the basin. Not that the spillage mattered; the whole interior of the boat looks as if it had been in a shower of light rain. What puzzles me is where it comes from. I even found water inside a big tin of Nivea which had been shut in the heads cupboard.

I'm excited to see how much the yacht does in the 24

hours starting from last night when I set the genoa. So far at 1625 hrs. the log is reading 456 which means 133 miles since 2015 last night with nearly four hours to go. A week of this pace would do me a lot of good.

I must have another shot at a radio beacon fix. I couldn't get any beacon this morning due to interference or background noise. I don't think it was the set because I picked up the BBC Light wavelength quite clearly. Tomorrow I must dig out the sextant. An astro fix is quicker than a radio one and much more accurate but I always put off using a sextant as long as possible, because of the different acts involved in taking and reducing a sight.

I shall never forget my humiliation and loss of face when on my first Royal Ocean Racing Club's race, crewing in the club's hell ship *Griffin I*, after being continuously seasick for thirty hours, I forgot to allow for the semi-diameter of the sun and we turned up at the Casquets off Alderney instead of at Guernsey.

But first I must light the good Aladdin stove. The fog makes the air damp and chilly.

17 June. 0909 hrs. What a ride we had last night! Holy smoke! Was it rough going! I confess I was apprehensive and anxious. The set-up was this: thick fog, or thick enough on a black night, 75-yard to 50-yard visibility, plenty of wind and a rough sea.

At 1900 hrs. a steamer passed me, foghorning at intervals. I replied with two toots of my little mouth horn at short intervals to show I was under sail on the port tack. I judge it was a big fast liner though I saw nothing whatever of it. Fast, because I was doing 7 knots and it still passed very quickly; big because its horn seemed very high; a liner because – no, I can't say why, just a fancy perhaps.

I felt a bit queasy, but dined off new potatoes and an onion with some mango chutney; nothing else and I think it was the right food. I took two Sea-legs.

At dusk I lit the powerful Tilley light and planted it on the counter where it must show up the sails sharply, and we charged into the night. It got rougher and I wondered if I ought to change to a smaller jib. However, I turned in and began sleeping heavily. Yet I don't think I slept more than ten minutes at a time between 2330 and 0125.

Rough going! It certainly was. The table woke me most often. It is built like a book hung by the spine and with lead instead of page edges. The two covers are the flaps which open up and are jammed horizontal when required. As the boat lurched one of the flaps would be left behind as the table swung. Sometimes the lurch to one side would be countered almost immediately by a lurch to the other side, very fast like a whip cracking. The table flap still swinging one way would be met by the table coming back and would give a mighty crack.

As it got rougher the yacht seemed to climb a wave, rush up it and pig-jump off the crest, landing with a terrific splash. The noise was appalling down below and one marvels at the strength of the boat. That's fair enough but the jumps made the table jump up in the sockets on which it pivots and land with an unholy din.

I kept on waking and feeling scared that the gear would not stand the strain, mast and sails principally. The build of a yacht simply amazes me. She was heeled 30° generally but with a good lurch heeled over to 50°. Imposed on that strain was the pig-jumping, leaping into a trough or being struck by a wave, now from one side and next from the other.

I was vacillating; several times I started out of the berth to change down the genoa. I pictured myself mastless. Then I'd tell myself the yacht was designed for this ocean sailing. (Another fog horn, 1008. A slow one toot: it passed well away to starboard. I could hear the horn plainly from the cabin long before I could hear it from the deck.)

Off I'd go to sleep only to be woken a few minutes later by another crack. Seeing a sea land on the inner side of the genoa worried me. It is cut low at the foot which curves round nearly down to deck level for 21 feet. The power of a sea bursting on this from the weather side must be very great. I was not worried about it dipping in the sea, which it frequently did, because that only pushed it in against the wind.

I kept on thinking of Sheila who said my chief trouble in this race would be carrying too much sail too long. On the other hand the yacht was sailing magnificently, really racing, the seas rushing past. I hated to slow her down. Finally at 0125 after a heavy sea came aboard I got up and dressed fully for foredeck work. I would change down the jib.

I put on oilskin trousers, long coat, sea-stopping towel scarf, cap, knife, spanner, torch (all three around my neck) and safety-belt ready for the fray. When I got into the cockpit she was sailing as well as she ever could and I hated to reduce sail. I stood and waited for the next sea but we must have sailed out of a rough patch just as I came on deck. From then on it was just fine sailing. I pumped up the Tilley, returned to my bunk and slept soundly till woken by a calm at 0530.

So ended a sail that I feel may be hard for me to beat single-handed: 220 miles from 2015 of the 15th to 0530 of the 17th; 33 hours 15 minutes at 6·6 knots.

Now to work. (1) I must rig an aerial and try to contact some of my pals of the transatlantic flight. (2) I've lost two battens out of the mainsail and ought to lower it to replace with makeshift ones. I'm afraid otherwise the incessant flapping, almost vibration, of the mainsail leach will start the stitching there. (3) I must have a good look at all the vane gear, for chafe or strain. That was another worry I had last night. When the yacht lurched, the rudder, which has 10 square feet of surface, would crash to one side pulling the wind vane violently with it. This is an unfair strain and I see that several of the wire stays of the vane have stretched or pulled their splicing. On the other hand it may be a good thing to have plenty of play in the vane for just that snatching by the rudder. Maybe I ought to feed in lengths of shock-cord to the tiller-lines.

Then (4) I must work up the DR position and get the sextant ready in the hope of sun and horizon being visible.

18th June. 1350 hrs. If anyone lacks interest, exercise or excitement or suffers in any way from boredom this is the answer. The only thing to mar it is the radio. I got the aerial rigged yesterday morning and have been listening in at stipulated moments since then. I heard a clipper of

Pan Am calling the race yachts once but he did not hear my reply. With a range of 100 miles or so it is very difficult to make contact with a 500-m.p.h. plane somewhere over the Atlantic.

1433 hrs. Sorry, I was overpowered by sleep. I listened in at 1400 and called up the clipper as requested but no reply.

I found to my astonishment that yesterday was Friday, and that I would have been out a week today and I know Sheila and Chris Brasher were expecting news from me by now. I tried calling up any steamer within sound-range but no answer. I think it is just not in the cards for me to get through a report of my position. Apart from the radio worry and a bad little accident which occurred this morning and which I will come to presently I wouldn't swap places with anyone in the world.

Yesterday was fine with plenty of fog. Occasionally the fog cleared and twice it lifted enough to show a horizon and the sun visible through the mist. I took advantage of these two clearings to get sextant shots at the sun, so at last got a fix. I had had none since the radio fix of two days before.

Fog, fog, fog wreathing over the waves and the long ocean swell. (I only realized what a long swell there was when it temporarily cleared.) The radio beacon went out of range on the 15th, three days ago. The sun fix put me at 50° 10′ N. 16° W. at 1815. I was glad to find this was only a few miles from the dead reckoning position worked up from the start six days ago. One would expect this when racing with a crew of good helmsmen but after all one can't ask Miranda what course she has been steering when one wakes up after several hours' sleep.

All day we kept going on the right course at speeds varying from 3½ to 6¼ knots. The wind gradually backed until at 2135, when I retrimmed the sails and Miranda, it had backed to south. I slept till 2330 when I got up and lit Tilley. I woke again at 0130 and found the boat becalmed and the sails slatting.

I topped up Miranda's spanker so that she should not bash into the backstay. I hardened in the main sheet to keep the main boom from banging from side to side, and, feeling guilty, crept back to my berth. Racing with a crew one would tend the sails all the time to take advantage of the faintest breeze. I was too sleepy to care.

At 0535 I awoke to find a light breeze. *Gipsy M* was hove-to headed north-east and fore-reaching slowly with the genoa aback. It took me quite a while to get the sails and wind vane trimmed. With the wind aft of the beam it is quite a tricky setting. I wasn't helped by the racing-flag being fouled again so that I could not see how the wind was at the masthead.

Then came my little bit of woe. Trying to shake the flag clear it came away from the burgee staff. I saw something fall in a fluttering heap into the sea like a collapsed blue pigeon. When I thought of all the loving care and craftsmanship put into making it by Sheila, my heart sank. She thought she had used better and more durable stuff, nylon-fortified; but always it seemed to be catching up in the masthead and did not fly so lightly as bunting does. It was already much frayed by the gale.

I sadly brought out the RORC burgee and hoisted that. The flag accident made me miss a listening period at 0630 for a BOAC plane. The wind was steadily backing and was now SE. with the result that I could not head better than 240°, which was 50° off the desired course. Pointing any closer to the required course would mean tangling Miranda's boom with the end of the main boom. Where would I be without Miranda? I must set twin spinnakers.

That was a big job especially as I had not done it before. I never got a chance to practise the operation. So I decided to have breakfast first. I laid a good foundation for the morning's work with a fry-up of potatoes and eggs – only two this morning – followed by the usual toast and coffee. It took me 1¾ hours to think out and get the gear ready and to boom out the genoa (already set).

Handling the 14-foot spinnaker boom requires careful forethought when attaching it to a 400-square-foot sail drawing well. I had to splice up two strops to attach the spinnaker booms to the tacks of the sails. Then I had to lower and furl the main sail. In the process the main boom flew out abeam. Something had carried away – dreaded sight for a racing sailor. But it turned out to be only a shackle at the boom-end carrying one of the blocks for the main sheet tackle. I nobbled the boom with a rope-end thrown over it and bowsed it down before any damage was done.

So far I only had one of the twins set. But setting the other from scratch was much easier. I clipped the second spinnaker boom to the clew of the sail before hoisting the sail and brought the boom up with the sail, a trick of Tom Worth's which I had read about.

Now they are both set and looking like a giant white sting ray hanging from the sky. The total area of the twins is 600 square feet. The setting of the genoa was definitely tricky; because of the size and length of the sail, the boom must be right aft against the shroud or else there is too much belly in the sail and it is apt to wallop the air in a drunken manner.

Robert Clark said I wouldn't be able to take it in again and he has more experience than almost any other yachtsman bar perhaps Olin and Rod Stephens of the USA and John Illingworth. I hope the wind does not get up stormy before I put his words to the test. However 'forewarned' etc. and I must think up some way of smothering it when I want to hand it.

1530 hrs. The old sting ray – giant manta really – hanging by his sting to the mast is still drawing fine. Quietly the log ticked off 6 nautical miles during the past hour. We roll considerably but sailors don't care as long as they're on the way. It was wonderful this morning working up in the stem with the scrunch of the bows shearing through the water, the soothing gurgle of the bow waves, the deep clear colour of the water.

I suppose I ought to go and repair the main boom ready in case it is needed suddenly for a wind shift. But I'm not going to; I'm going to have another sleep.

By the way, when I looked at the log it read 698 miles. Considering it wasn't set for six hours at the start and was out of action for an unknown length of time when fouled by the yacht going round in circles one night while I was sleeping, and considering the gales and squalls at the start ... the head winds, the fact that I missed a lot of chances

73

through lack of skill the first few days, I say, considering all this, we are not doing too badly.

2310 hrs. I'm usually very thorough about washing-up. At least that's my view. My wife for some reason quite beyond me thinks entirely the opposite. The point is that I overlooked washing up my glass so the only sensible thing to do with it, considering the need for saving fuel, is, instead of heating up another lot of wash-up water, to fill it with whisky and water and sit down for a chatter.

One has heard it said that people who live alone talk to themselves. As I have been talking aloud today I wondered if the saying was true. I think it is wrong. One is not talking to oneself but thinking aloud. If I could sing I would, but I can't. If I try to sing the note of a bird for example something is emitted which would appear to resemble the moan of a rhinoceros with acute indigestion.

Time after time I have tried to call up a ship or an aircraft and have listened in in case anyone should be calling us. Not that it matters to me failing to make contact; the radio mars the serenity of an adventure like this. But having a radio telephone aboard, I worry that Sheila and my friends will worry if they hear nothing of me. I don't think Sheila would, really, because she has such faith in me and even if something went wrong she would regard it as destined and decreed rather than worry lest it could have been prevented.

I must change position. Countering the rolling and bracing myself to avoid being pitched off my seat is making my back ache. An additional cushion behind and feet against the opposite settee should make it easier.

I got pitched across the cabin while lighting a lamp and knocked my whisky over. (You might think I would fill it again, but I had put the bottle away so I won't.) That's the only drawback to running with twins set and no mainsail to steady the roll. She rolls pretty fast from side to side and its a bit tricky if you have your hands full or are caught off balance. I hit my chest against something exactly where I had the big blow the other day. It was really painful for a while. Before that, it has hurt me if I cough and gets very stiff while I'm asleep. I certainly gave it a good dint the other day.

74

Sitting in the cabin I can hear the bow waves form as if breaking and then rush along the hull, gurgling and seething. It is delightful running. This is the first real run I've had in *Gipsy Moth* since she was built. None of that chilly wind and spray that you get when on the wind. All day I have left her alone except to retrim the helm and Miranda. Since I set the twins she has quietly gone ahead with no fuss or noise averaging 6 knots; she has knocked off 54 miles in the nine hours. I suppose she would do 8 to 9 knots with the spinnaker (850 square feet) and the mainsail (380 square feet) but I could not leave the helm with a spinnaker set and the gain for a few hours' steering would be lost in setting and handing it every time.

I had to leave the helm. There is a lot to do besides helmsmanship. This afternoon I fitted a new shackle to the main boom sheet tackle and tautened up both the fore and aft lower shrouds on both sides – a lengthy job fiddling with the split pins which I wanted to save, having no replacements.

I only hope this breeze holds for a day or two; it does make life easy. And it is blowing directly to New York, which is helpful. I shall turn in tonight without a worry. Now I must go and fill the Tilley lamp before hanging it in the stern.

I found a moth on the after deck yesterday. Surely that might be a good omen. I took it very carefully into the cabin and settled it on a port light. I hope it has enough sense to sit there and not try to fly ashore. I have not seen it again but there are any number of good crannies for it to hide in. It was not a gipsy moth but it hardly could be since that kind is extinct in Europe, and exists only in North America I believe.

Marvellous sailing. Hard to beat. The fog has cleared at last even if only temporarily. The breeze, east, Force 4, seems to be holding well.

CHAPTER SIX

June 19th to 21st

A Worrying Night under the Twins – One Pole Adrift
– Repairs – Close Hauled again – On Course for Cape
Race! – Steamer Lane and Ice – Line of Squalls –
Gybe! – What Price Cleanliness? – Dirty Weather on
Way – Sad News about the Moth – The Eye of the
Depression – Man and Boat – Haggis with Accessories
– The Chocolate Hoard – Poor Red Bucket!

19th June. 1345 hrs. Just finishing off lunch with mush-rooms on buttered toast and would like to have a little chat so I bring out the book.

In the end it wasn't the starboard spinnaker pole which came adrift but the port one. But perhaps I am a bit ahead of my preamble. I started a marvellous sleep at midnight (it was about eighty minutes before midnight here really because of the longitude west) and was drugged with sleep when I started worrying about the strop linking the big genoa to the starboard spinnaker pole. It was only experimental, and I had made it of 1-inch manila rope not thinking the twins would be set for so long. This woke me up and I went on to think what would happen if the spinnaker boom did break loose. I realized I had only stayed it from above, i.e. had it topped up from its middle to a point higher up the mast. It would be free to swing from side to side and the thought of a 14-foot pole about 18 inches in circumference in the middle bashing from side to side with the ship rolling through an arc of 60° (30° each side of vertical) was not conducive to peaceful slumber.

I got up and dressed fully plus boots this time as I visualized a bit of climbing. It was drizzling and as black as pitch. It makes the stem of a yacht a romantic spot with the forefoot crashing through the sea and the thundery cascade of the bow-wave seeming as loud as a big steamer's.

By standing on the top life-line round the ship I could just reach the middle of the spinnaker boom and I clipped on two preventer guys which I cleated to the deck fore and aft of the pole. It was now held from three directions and I felt relieved. I looked a little wistful at the other boom to port but the No. 2 (225 square feet) jib seems fairly harmless compared with the genoa and I return to my berth at three o'clock and slept hard till eight o'clock.

After breakfast I was doing odd jobs below when I thought the short steep sea must have changed to make the hull shake and the oil stove tinkle. In the end I went up to look at it and there was the port spinnaker boom swinging to and fro hitting the forestay at one end of its travel and a lower shroud at the other. After all, it was not the rope strop which had parted but the spring-held pin which closes the hook at the end of the pole which had come adrift.

Light airs made it an easy job yet it took nearly the whole morning. There are a surprising lot of operations involved when the gear is big and only one pair of hands available: nobble the pole, lower it, lower the sail, brail it at the middle, repair the fitting (fetch various tools); prepare fore and aft down-guys for boom preventers, splice an eye at the end of one with a sailmaker's whipping at the other end; work boom into position again from lying on deck. Hoist all and trim the sheet plus topping lift plus two guys. Retire satisfied.

Working up the DR position filled the rest of the morning. From noon to noon we ran 130·4 miles under the twins and mostly while I was asleep. Our noon position was 49° 41′ N. 20° 45′ W. and the best course for New York 264° true.

Now I must fit some old battens into the mainsail and do some sewing which I think will keep them in. Without them the leach of the sail shudders continually so that in time the stitching must give way. Also I must oil the log – reading 809 at noon – but I shall be sorry to quieten its friendly little note. It builds up an accumulation of turns on the line, until the instrument starts off spinning madly, making an attractive whicker like teal flighting into a pond at dusk.

2330 hrs. The sun has just gone down in a nearly cloudless sky – a very clear sky as the sea is a clear deep blue – the breaking bow-wave is a dazzling clear white by contrast. What a change! All the afternoon the wind backed steadily. The twins still drove the boat but I could see I must get a move on to be ready for a change-over. I fitted two old battens of plastic in place of those lost in the mainsail and put what I hope were well-placed stitches through the sail to prevent their being joggled out by the slatting sail. The others were lost when lowering the main in a gale.

I seized afresh a mainsail slide to the sail, the old seizing having carried away. I sat astride the boom to do it and could see a hard-cut horizon far away, a big change after days of fog and bad weather. It was even drying weather for an hour or two and I bustled a few damp things out but I had too much else on my hands for much of that.

By the time I had finished make-and-mend the wind was far enough round to let Miranda take charge with the mainsail set. Of course the main can be set any time but I cannot risk Miranda fully set, spanker and all, if the wind is so far round that there is a chance of the main boom crashing into her.

The number of jobs involved in a change-over from running to close-hauled is annoying. Apart from hoisting the main which would be up already with a full-crewed racer there were two booms to unrig and hand to the deck, to be lashed down at both ends, and their topping lifts to be cleated up. One twin remains set and the unwanted twin has to be unhanked and bagged. Another sheet transferred to the genoa. Then of course there was the sail trimming and setting of Miranda which still takes half an hour of watching though I am learning her foibles pretty fast.

Now we are scurrying along on course for the turning-point south of Cape Race Newfoundland. *Gipsy M.* knocked off 24½ miles in the last four hours although there does not seem much more than a light breeze. She has that

78

trick of shaking her tail like a fish. It gives one a feeling of
– I can't get the word to describe it – being woggled. It
seems very innocent and quiet but it catches you off
balance and throws you easily.

I must go and rig a lamp. We are in or very close to the
main New York–Liverpool steamer lane, the normal one
for this time of year. But the ice is much farther north this
year so the steamers will be cutting Newfoundland closer.
It seems to be an exceptionally good year for ice and I
could not be more pleased. If there is one thing I like less
than fog to sail through it is fog stuffed with ice.

20 June. 1300 hrs. At last I'm up in the cockpit for my little
gossip. Since the sun came out I've been working hard to
get up here and now it is hazing over and I've missed my
chance I fear.

Last night I turned in and had a good sleep confident
that with Miranda and Tilley in charge the boat was in
good hands. I should think Tilley could be seen 10 miles
away from a high steamer's bridge but I have not worked
it out. No, I think the bridge would have to be 75 feet
high; however, I can say 5 miles confidently. Apart from
a tour of the deck at 0300 I slept till 0830 when I woke to
find the wind had gone round to the south and Miranda
had followed it as instructed, so that we were heading
240°, or 45° off New York. I went on deck to find a line of
squalls passing through.

I tried to trim up to get on course – immediately I was
in the cockpit. This was a stupid thing to do. I might know
by now how sluggish-witted I am for a few minutes after
getting out of the berth. While my back was turned (and
bent) re-setting Miranda's vane arms, the yacht ran off
downwind and gybed. Boom over. Genoa aback. Miranda
coming round fast to be in peril from a gybe back of the
main boom or if she escaped that one, in danger of coming
up with her spanker boom hard against the backstay.

For a while I was like a monkey on a hot trapeze.
Seriously handicapped by having been caught bent double
with my head down to the deck fiddling with the clamp at
the bottom of Miranda's rotating mast. I was disoriented
and could not take in for a few seconds what the direction

79

was in which the yacht was turning, where the wind was coming from and which way Miranda would swing if we continued turning as we were.

I jumped back into the cockpit and related these things one by one to the compass, steadied the yacht nearly straight downwind, hopped back to the counter and released Miranda, pushed her by brute force away from the backstay and gybed her; then back to the tiller and sorted out the tangle step by step.

It was a fair squall of wind and heavy rain by now, and I took over the helm for a while, looking round with some distaste at the various squalls in sight. I dreaded the wind going astern so that I should have all the toil of resetting the twin spinnakers. I was relieved when it backed to south and I could trim up for a broad reach. Yet this is a tricky heading for Miranda. The helm does not require a heavy hand if the sails are trimmed to a true balance so long as the heading is within say 15° of what everything has been set for. If, however, for some reason, like a quick change of wind strength or a ponderous sea, she gets off course 30–40° to leeward she starts galloping off to leeward and it takes a strong arm to force her back.

This is above Miranda's head. She can't understand why she should need only the velvet glove one minute and the iron mitt the next. In the end sails and vane were in harmony and the yacht kept within 260° and 310° weaving from one side to the other. After an hour of monitoring I felt confident enough to go below and get on with my housework.

Just then the sun came out and the day appeared bright and clear. I think it must have been a mild trough of low pressure passing through. I took the opportunity of a sextant shot at the sun which would give me a longitude, the sun being due east. Breakfast at last at 1000 hrs. Ham and eggs with fry-up of potatoes. Toast, marmalade and coffee. At least starvation should not rear its ugly head for a few hours. It was warm and summery in the cockpit and I wanted to be there but alas my conscience did me down. I felt the time had come for a top-half wash cum shave. One really needs to be an acrobat to achieve these things with G.M. bashing out her steady 6 knots but I managed to get through with only one sharp blow on the forehead from the edge of the cupboard opening. I have to open this cupboard to get my head over the basin.

I was somewhat worried about an attack in the rear. I could only maintain position by pressing my backside against the door jamb. The door was open because I did not want to be caught again by its bursting open and throwing me across the alley way. What I was scared of now was that it would slam shut and pinch a piece of my tender loin between door and door jamb.

It is really a two-way door which either shuts on the heads or when open to the heads shuts off the forecabin from the main cabin. Unfortunately the naval wireless P/O who fixed the aerial for my R/T did not realize about the door's second position and ran the aerial through the doorway thus effectively preventing the door from being kept open to the heads.

The result of all this crazy rage for cleanliness is that the weather had deteriorated by the time I reached the cockpit and I was glad to get under cover again, my sun-bask changed to a wash-out.

I fear dirty weather is on the way and must get my battledress on.

1705 hrs. Here I am back again to finish the whisky I was drinking at 1415 while writing the above. Never a dull moment, I say. Did I say it before? It looks as if it is likely to be a regular cropper-upper.

What did I achieve in that hurly-burly? Dashed little – I got the genoa down as the squall pounced. It wasn't too bad; in fact rather fun. Once the boat pitched and threw me off the deck into the air at the bows. I went up in the air and landed back again, surprised. I expect it was only a millimetre jump but it is the sensation that counts.

I bagged up the genoa. One of the things I've learned this voyage is how to bag a foresail with a minimum of effort and dolour; I drag it along the deck like a dead snake and bag it as it arrives, ramming it in small folds.

I set No. 3 jib, a little 'un. Not for its drive but because the boat can not be handled with main only in a strong blow in a seaway. I thought I was doing pretty well about keeping dry and felt quite cocky when another sea gave

81

me a good sluice where I was sitting by the mast making up the halliards. My oilskin (PVC really) outfit seemed pretty good when suddenly a nasty cold icicle made itself unpleasantly felt in a quiet spot of the body particularly sensitive to cold water. Part of the sea had remained in my lap where I sat and found its way through the gap there.

I sailed the boat myself for a while. The wind had come nearly dead aft and the boat was tricky to handle with the main set. Yet I couldn't sit there, at the helm all day. I couldn't think of any way to handle the situation except by getting down the main. Unless I kept running downwind, there was too much wind for it and not only did it flap but it was making the boat hard to control. So it had to come down. That seemed a fairly easy operation this time. One does seem to learn pretty fast at this game. I began to work out how I could set the twin spinnakers again.

Then I noticed that the wind was backing once more. So then I thought how I'd hate to set those twins to find they weren't wanted two hours later and finally I called it a half-holiday and retired for some lunch and a drink which I am now enjoying very much indeed, thank you.

Meanwhile, the boat under one small jib and in the charge of a reefed Miranda is at least sailing in the right direction if only at a mere knot or two. I'm quite prepared to find we are becalmed by the time I've finished my whisky and cheese.

2145 hrs. Well, I don't know, but I reckon there's been enough of this weather for a while. The cabin sole is piling up with wet clothes. God only knows what beds of fungi and mildew are flourishing under the unused berths.

I finished my lunch and a zizz at 1900 hrs. and decided to set the trysail. For one thing rolling through an arc of 80° would be reduced by a trysail. Secondly it looked as if the rough weather had set in. It was blowing Force 6 or 7 so a main was not feasible. I finished setting the trysail at 2040 hrs. It is not such a bad job if one sets about it step by step and does not get fussed. I have two hefty tackles port and starboard to control the clew and another to downhaul the tack. The chief trouble was that the halliard was in use to hoist the aerial of the radio-telephone. It is amazing how that aerial has been an obstacle. Every time I move along the deck I have to step over it or under it, and now hauling it down with two huge glass insulators flying about adds to the fun. The log reads 1001. I tallied up the day's runs since the start, going by the log which I have previously found accurate. The distances sailed are:

June 12th – 88; 13th – 43; 14th – 101; 15th – 72; 16th – 147; 17th – 144½; 18th – 106; 19th – 130½; 20th – 150.

I added on the first day the distance sailed before the log was streamed. I wonder if my rivals are getting this bad weather. I hope not for their sakes; it can't be much fun in a sea like this in a folkboat.

Sad news; I found the moth dead. I fear he had stowed away among the gear and been hit by its shifting during the rolls. Equally sad that I had prepared a surprise for dinner tonight, but it doesn't look a joyful antic trying to cook. I opened a parcel yesterday and found it was from a Scots friend, Stalker Miller, an artist who draws a lot of maps for us. He had sent me two haggises. It seems to me a bold enterprise to undertake one and definitely it should be done before the Scotch gives out.

No, I think tonight the menu will be two Sea-legs and a glass of whisky. A grey outlook, grey mist, grey sky, grey seas. I must go and secure that damn aerial. I can hear it sculling round the deck. It will be chasing me down here unless I muzzle it. Pass the bottle, please.

21st June. 1015 hrs. I slept till eight o'clock. Now and then I heard sounds which indicated we were becalmed. That one should hear anything was surprising, above the terrific din of bottles clinking, pots and pans, plates, tins, cutlery, various boxes, objects sliding from side to side in cupboards. Later I was aware of a breeze and things quietened down in the cabin.

I woke feeling guilty and was shamed by the boat, ticked off for not pressing on. How? Because we were still headed west but with the wind from the north instead of from the south. I left her with jib aback and trysail drawing to a south wind, headed west and it was a bit uncanny to wake seven or eight hours later to find her still travelling west but with the jib drawing and the trysail aback to a north wind. She had sailed on her way 12½ miles during the night.

However, I was glad to find that my guess forecast of the weather had been right. We had sailed into the eye of the depression with the wind south before entering the calm eye and north on leaving it. On the whole I did the right thing but a keen racing type would have got up at five when the north breeze arrived instead of lazing in idle sleep till eight.

I found the sea nearly calm, the sky clear in parts with some dark storm cloud in the distance which might mean more trouble. It took me 1 hour 20 minutes to hand and bag the trysail, sort out all its tackles, remove the various preventers which kept the main boom from swinging about and hoist and set the mainsail. It was a big effort to get it up with the wind on the beam making the slides stick, the sail press against the shrouds and battens catch up in the rigging.

How it is being driven home that this race is man and boat and not just boat! The Viking will lose no time with his sail-setting or gear-handling where I use many hours.

I am full of moans this morning. I felt desperate struggling with the mainsail, my hands are unpleasantly tender with the skin and nails worn thin handling gear; everything in the boat seems to be damp if not wet. I have the Aladdin stove going full blast.

I went on strike and said 'Breakfast and coffee before setting the genoa.' Sigh; my break is over. By the way, what am I moaning about; the one thing I was worrying about, my chest, which had become very painful coughing or handling gear, seems better this morning. And the sun is shining.

1625 hrs. I caught sight of that last sentence. The sun certainly did not shine for long. I set the genoa and trimmed the sails and Miranda to keep the required heading. Setting Miranda to the required 5 or 10 degrees seems to take me ½ to 1 hour on a fresh tack. It seems to require more handling than the sail trimming.

I used valuable sun-time in oiling the piston hanks of

the No. 3 jib which were real finger-biters, so that when I got out the sextant I just got the sun down to the horizon when the overcast hid it completely. However it was not a vital matter. Although I like knowing exactly where I am, it is not essential in mid-Atlantic. It was my own fault anyway, because I saw the frontal overcast sky approaching.

By 1240 I was pretty hungry and determined to treat myself to the big surprise, the haggis. I'm not sure what goes with it but I put on some potatoes and onions and laid out what I'm certain no good Scot would eat it without – a bottle of Scotch.

As soon as all this was fairly under way I realized that the genoa was overpowering the boat so I dressed fully and changed it to No. 2 jib. Surprising how little the wind was as soon as the genoa was off compared with the bluster with it set, the ominous thunder of the leach shaking, the whines in the rigging.

I'm afraid this interlude may have overcooked the haggis but it was very good and most interesting. I pondered on what fine tough people the Scots must be if they live on haggis!

Now I am reclining on my berth in sumptuous peace of mind and body hardly turning my head when a kettle flies across the cabin. The movement is certainly lively, we are on our way again. I shall have to go up for a retrim soon. I see by the tell-tale compass at the end of the table that we are 30° off course south of west which shows the wind is steadily backing.

On second thought, retrimming would hardly gain another 10° on the wind because the jib is shaking already when she comes up to 270°. She wanders through an arc of 20–30°, in this case 250 to 275°, whereas the heading I want is 285°. I expect the wind to shoot round to sw. soon, when I shall have to tack. I think I might as well have a little indolent ease meanwhile.

At last I have found the chocolate hoard. I've made several attempts to locate it but every likely spot seemed filled with David Lewis's first-aid and medical supplies. I ran into a box of streptomycin under the starboard pilot berth mattress with a most impressive assortment of medical specialities. I tried under the covering of the port berth and ran into two sun-stills for distilling fresh water out of salt by using sun-heat.

In the forecabin I was baulked by a large dump of emergency rations on one berth and a huge red box of lifeboat distress signals in the other. In another drawer I ran into David's tin of anti-shark powder.

I have still had no contact with anyone since leaving Plymouth and hope Sheila won't be worrying. I can't do anything today about the R/T because I can't hoist the aerial on the port side while the mainsail is set there on this tack. I have not seen a ship since the fishing smack *L'Inconnu*[1] woke me up early after the start of the race.

I'm surprised to see that yesterday's run was 80 miles sailed when we seemed to be in difficulty the whole time with bad weather. I suppose we were scuttling along pretty fast with the strong wind astern even when we had nothing but the small jib up.

I lost the red gash bucket overboard this morning when I was emptying it. It looked very cocky sitting scarlet on the surface. I was sorry to see it go.

I've got an awful lot of jobs I ought to do but I'm tired. Handling the sails in a strong wind builds up to hard work. Thank heaven the sky looks brighter seen from where I indolentolate in my berth. Bong! That landed on the cabin top with much noise.

[1] My log, June 12th at 1100 hrs., records that I was woken by *L'Inconnu Camaret* which came alongside in a rough sea with visibility very bad. She was obviously intending to board *Gipsy Moth*. No doubt she thought she had a nice piece of salvage of an abandoned yacht. The crew looked very surly when I appeared and they disregarded my waving as they quickly sheered off and went in the opposite direction.

CHAPTER SEVEN

June 22nd to 25th

The Mysterious Vessel – Miranda at Work – Over-
canvassed – Gale – The Other Miranda – China Tea
and Cake – Third of the Voyage – Slim Chances of
Winning – Vikings and Ravens – Gastronomic Fan-
tasy – Crash in the Night – Another Gale – In Praise
of John Tyrrell – Tender Fingers and Fatigue – Depression – Seas 15 Feet High – Anything for Peace –
The Man with the Hosepipe – Sunshine – Under
Twins Again – The Life-line – Miranda Loses her
Grip

22nd June. It is hard to keep track of the date, there is so
much going on. What a sight for mad housewives ... what
a din when I went below at 1220, just past noon. The cabin
sole covered in papers, wet clothes, cordage, anything
loose in the boat. While the din was frightful ... every
bottle, jar, cup and plate, spoon or what-have-you crashing
from one side of its cupboard to the other. Kettles and
saucepans clanging, stowed tins clinking, water in the tank
below the cabin sole booming as it rushed from side to
side. The big No. 2 jib in its bag had attacked the Primus
and was impaled on the pump handle. Well, it was only the
effect of the rolling while I was on deck.

If we go on getting these violent changes of weather,
the Herculean Viking and my other rivals will be catching
me up. Look what's happened since I was last writing
yesterday afternoon. We went well at 7 knots all the afternoon, with the wind steadily backing through NW. to West.

A ship passed us but I made no attempt to signal her. I
waved at the chap on the bridge and then to the cook, I
think, looking over the stern. She was called CYAA. I don't
know what language that is but she looked very foreign, a
dirty rusty grey with a remarkable lot of radar and radio

gear on her mast aft. An open lattice work structure in the well-deck. I thought if I tried to signal she wouldn't understand and might come dangerously close.

For some reason I felt apprehensive as she passed. After drawing ahead she sheered across my bows and steamed ahead, obviously to find out the direction in which I was going. She could not know much about yachts. Otherwise she would know that the direction of a yacht is governed by the wind at the time.

I was equally curious about where she was going, which appeared to be Baffin Land or somewhere in that direction. She looked like a tanker, but a tiny one. I wondered if she was a submarine refuelling ship or perhaps a rocket missile spotter. Only about 1,500 tons I estimated.

By 2100 hrs. the wind had fallen light and I changed jibs again, setting the genoa. I went to sleep. The wind continually backing and Miranda following it faithfully, I awoke at 2300 hrs. to find we were nearly headed south. So I tacked but after that I could not get her to go again. She hung about pointing northwards and refused to budge. Finally in disgust I went below. A few minutes later I noted with surprise on the telltale compass that we were steady on our course, 295° compass and sailing quietly along. Evidently Miranda's way of showing me what a slacker I was!

The boat sailed 16 miles while I slept four hours when I awoke to find the wind had continued to back to SE. and we were again headed 220° but on the opposite (port) tack. I trimmed sails and vane gear, which took nearly an hour and again I slept. Gradually the wind grew stronger and stronger. I half woke and thought I ought to change to a smaller jib but slept on. *Gipsy M.* was racing through the night like a scalded cat. If she could take it, it was great racing. The going got rougher and rougher and I could hear the shaking leeches drumming hard which showed she was over-canvassed. But I turned over and slept on. Finally at 1000 hrs. I got up reluctantly; this riotous gallop must slow down. Meanwhile she had sailed 38 miles in the last 5½ hours. I soon put a stop to that progress. As soon as I handed the genoa, she stopped dead with the mainsail flogging.

It was now blowing up pretty hard and I tried to reef the main. It seemed a desperately tough job. Everything jammed or caught up. If I headed the boat into the wind the mainsail could be reefed easily enough but would flog itself to bits while the least wind I could keep in her to keep her quiet was too much for reefing because it pressed the sail against the shrouds and jammed the slides in their track.

I did get two reefs rolled down, but the wind increased faster than I could reef. It was blowing a gale by now. Finally I gave up reefing and lowered the whole sail. By now even this had become quite a job. As soon as the sail was down the boom began swinging from side to side and must be hobbled before it caused havoc.

At the critical moment the topping lift uncleated itself and let the boom onto the life-line round the ship. But luck was with me. I caught the flying part of the topping lift before it disappeared in the sky above and I hauled on it to lift the boom off the life-line while I hauled on the main-sheet at the same time to clamp down the swinging boom. What a murderous weapon that boom can be!

Finally I set a small jib, got the yacht onto her heading, cleaned up the mess of cordage and wire littering the deck and cockpit and went below where I then enjoyed a very good breakfast. Meanwhile the wind has been dropping as I write so I suppose I must see about more sail change.

No, I can hear that high-pitched whine in the rigging above the cacophony of pots and pans, so perhaps I shall be justified in leaving her plodding westwards with only a small jib. I do think this continued bad weather is out of season. It is midsummer today but I have not succeeded in drying a single bit of clothing for ten days. However, we did knock out 121 miles yesterday in spite of the calm and wildly changing winds. The log reads 1,162 miles to date.

If only it would calm down a bit I could rig the aerial and make some more attempts to send a message; we are on the right tack for setting it but it is a great toil to rig anything in these conditions.

Later I popped up quickly for a look-see and was quite pleased to find it still blowing pretty hard from the south. Plenty of whine in the rigging. Visibility about 200 yards in the mist. The sea appears to be blown flat but it can't be really. Otherwise we should not have this rolling. I retrimmed to get back on the right heading. We have averaged only 3⅓ knots while I have been below and a hardy type would set a trysail. But not this chicken, thank you. Twice I've set the damn thing this trip and it takes more stuffing out of me than changing ten headsails.

Trysail conditions only seem to last a few hours and I think it will be good policy to sacrifice the extra two knots and keep nice and fresh for putting the mainsail back immediately conditions are suitable for it. With that trysail caper, I am so fagged out that I delay resetting the main and the operation takes three times as long when there is a trysail with tackles to clear away first. Have I proved to your satisfaction that another little zizz is the best policy before taking any next step?

1610 hrs. By this time I have the mainsail fully reefed, set and drawing very nicely. I had a little snooze after breakfast and read a few pages about Miranda in *The Tempest*, which I enjoy just as much for the hundredth reading. After that I felt in fettle again and had no trouble at all in finishing off reefing the main, hoisting and trimming it. Wind still Force 6, visibility bad, 200 yards in mist and drizzle. A few seas hit us though the sea looks moderate.

One sea fairly startled me; it was exactly like a bomb of the 1939 war exploding, and not too far away; the boat jumped and shook – or perhaps I did! But there was no malice in it. I think old Neptune forgets his power at times and was just giving us a friendly slap on the buttock as if saying, 'On with you, fellow, get cracking and good luck.' Now I'm enjoying a cup of Earl Grey China tea and hoeing into the delicious cake Mrs Buckmaster, our housekeeper, made for me. I should love to see her face and hear what she would say if her kitchen suddenly tipped up 50°. Shall I finish the cake or leave one slice for tomorrow?

I am using far more paraffin than I expected. Tilley takes a bottle a night, and I have had the stove (Aladdin) going quite a lot trying to dry out the cabin and warm it, with the damp clammy fog about. Then there are my three cabin-lamps and the riding-light, Old Faithful.

Last night when it was clear I set Old Faithful in the stern instead of Tilley, which means a big saving of fuel, but I like to have Tilley out there when visibility is bad. Her light is very powerful and should be a good protection against being run down. On a clear night I think it would be a mistake because any ship seeing it might wonder what was happening and come scraping alongside if I was asleep.

I must pop out and see what speed we are making with the reefed main and small jib. With the small jib only we were doing 3¾ knots – modest but better than nothing and in the right direction. 1,181½ on the log at 1722 hrs., 6½ miles in 72 minutes makes 5½ knots. I suppose that is as much as one could expect from the set-up.

Perhaps she might stand a bigger jib in an hour's time or so. The wind is abating. I must get the best speed I can, but I'm satisfied by now that the first consideration is to keep fresh and have a reserve of strength. If I bullock along when I'm exhausted I make silly decisions and take twice as long over a job as I would if fresh. If I have a difficult job to do when I'm fatigued, if it can possibly be deferred – which often it can't be in an emergency – I'll do the job better and quicker if I go and sleep for ten minutes first.

One of my chief reasons for speed is that I would dearly love to race Sheila across the Atlantic. She leaves England on the 26th (it was the 28th) on the French liner *Flandres*, which I believe does 21 knots. She should arrive therefore some time on July 2nd (it was the 5th).

I have done exactly one-third of my direct journey at noon today so if I keep up the same pace I should arrive July 14th. My chances of racing her, therefore, look remarkably slim. In fact I should need to travel at twice my pace up to date which is absurd. I've taken eleven days today, therefore will take thirty-three days at the same pace. If I can't arrive before the *Flandres*, I would dearly love to beat thirty days across. Quick! I must go and crack on some more sail!

1920 hrs. My luck's in tonight. It is still blowing Force 6 or thereabouts, and the whine in the rigging has a purposeful note not apparent below deck. The boat is going well with the present rig and has averaged 5·8 knots since I last

91

went up at 1722 hrs. I trimmed the mainsail a little but it is setting beautifully for a fully reefed sail. The wind is heading us and we are already 10° above the required course, but that can't be helped. I'd rather it stayed wsw. even if that prevents our making good our best course, than fly all round the compass requiring endless sail changes.

There is quite a lot of water hitting the decks. I pumped the bilges dry with fifty-two strokes. As this is only the second pump-out I've given her since the start it looks as if the hull is tight below the waterline which is all that really matters.

I shouldn't complain about everything being damp inside above the waterline. After all, the Vikings when they set out to discover America – Erik the Red and that lot – must have had a damn sight wetter living-quarters than I have. And they had to share theirs with some ravens too, which must have had some serious drawbacks in a small boat.

David Lewis, when sailing alone to Norway last year had a pigeon come aboard and stay. A seasick pigeon inside a Vertue for several days appals me. The extraordinary thing is that it laid an egg. David's friends say the pigeon did not realize David was only a GP and not a gynaecologist.

Where is the Guinness? I must do something about this Guinness; I have three cases aboard and am hardly half-way through one. I'm a bit wary of it when there is any serious deck work in prospect. Whether this export variety is specially gingered up (I had this lot out of bond as duty-free stores) I don't know, but I reckon that three small cans have the same effect as two-thirds of a bottle of whisky. With serious work in view, I drink whisky to keep my head clear.

Now for lunch; it looks as if I shall not get as far as dinner today. I wish I had a gastronomic epicure here to advise me. Last night I had a ham omelette. I find a well-cooked potato in its jacket hard to beat as a foundation.

I would like some grilled fresh salmon and fresh peas. What about new potatoes, a tin of French petits pois and some prawns – out of a tin, alas, but very nice. Tomato soup – no I had that last night, Mr Heinz's best (and delicious it was) but a whole tin tends to blunt the appetite. I think perhaps a little Danish blue with cream crackers and some nuts and raisins to top up with if desired. Put them on the menu anyway. After all it is midsummer night. How about a bottle of Burgundy for the occasion? No, perhaps not, it might make me think of the good companionship I am missing. I have never met anyone like Sheila for making a bottle of wine a great delight with her amusing and interesting companionship. I think she must be a Regency hostess come adrift from her century.

Damn! the jib is shaking. I fear Miranda is pinching her a trifle. (Later) Now we are going like a cat with a scalded tail. It is the wind piping up again. I hope we are not in for a really serious storm because if so I may regret my midsummer night's feast. Enough of this badinage – to the galley.

23rd June. 1030 hrs. Well, I certainly ought to laugh about what I wrote yesterday. All that nonsense about getting to New York quickly. It would be a pretty feeble ha-ha, though. My doleful tale is this: last night after an excellent dinner I went on deck full of booze and bonhomie and thought that (crazy loon!) although she was skittling along at 5·8 knots, she would skittle along even faster with a full main. So I promptly unrolled the whole of my nicely rolled-up reefing. I even pulled out a bigger jib but fortunately decided that would be too much of a good thing.

I went below and was half out of my oilskins preparatory to logging 1,212 miles at 2310 hrs., when there was the most thunderous crash. I felt, or thought I felt the boat sink under the weight of water. My heart went down with it. I dressed again and went on deck. I was intensely surprised to find the dinghy still there, still lashed down, and I was immensely pleased when I could find nothing carried away. Obviously it sounded much worse below. I suppose it is like being inside a drum and someone bashing the outside hard.

I could not have seen the red light quicker, we were going too fast for the sea running. I set to work and lowered and furled the main again. It went smoothly enough but it wasn't easy in the gale which by now was blowing. The main boom started swinging and hitting the weather runner which set me scrambling aft from the mast as fast as I could go. I hardened in the main sheet as fast as I could, ducking the boom as it swung and then tethered it firmly with another rope. I trimmed the shock-cord tiller lines, clocked in a topped-up Miranda and left the deck with just the small jib set. I went below and turned in.

It was a rough night. I must say how glad I am this boat was built by John Tyrrell. He is a member of the RORC, which you can't join without taking part in at least one of their races; in other words he knows what the boat is wanted for; but he builds fishing boats and lifeboats chiefly so also knows what a boat is up against in a storm.

I was chiefly worried about Miranda, comparatively delicate, getting strained, but she seems all right. We were hit by many seas but none worse than the one I described. I peeped up several times to see that all was well but otherwise slept till nine o'clock (seven o'clock local time) only forced awake then by a saucepan making a frightful din.

I was most reluctant to wake up and get out of my berth; but the boat had worked her way round to north and I wondered if there was anything I could do about it. I could not bring her up any closer to the wind under jib only. With a trysail she would come back to 340° or possibly 330° but even that is 40–50° off the course for New York. Is it worth all the trysail sweat or should I wait till the sea and wind abate and I can set the main again? If the sea and wind improve within three hours it will pay me to wait but if they continue bad for days I shall have blundered.

I am writing this because I think it will help me decide right. Every writer who has described a single-handed voyage has said that fatigue is the most serious hazard or implied it. I must confess that setting that big mainsail and the trysail in bad weather takes the ginger out of me. The big headsails I don't mind; they seem easy by comparison.

94

My fingers are so tender that I have difficulty in opening a tin and last night in the hurly-burly I stupidly let one of the cabin doors which snap shut pulled by shock-cord, snap shut on my fingers. This made me sit up and has given one fingernail the blues this morning to match my toe. As a matter of fact I felt I had been very lucky indeed to get off so lightly.

Hark at that wind whining! Surely not more storm. I wonder what my rivals are doing. I hope they did not catch this packet; last night I would think would be pretty good hell in a 5-tonner. But they could be only 200 miles away and miss a storm completely.

24th June. 1250 BST. As we are 33° west of Greenwich, the time here by the sun is two hours earlier.

I kept away from my little blue book confidant after I had written in the morning. I had the blues, the weather had the greys, I had too much to do, I was fagged out and I didn't like the set-up. I was apprehensive and jumpy. Being in a boat for 12 days with everything getting wetter every day and no chance to dry a single thing is a dampener of morale.

I turned my oilskin trousers inside out when it seemed set fine for half an hour yesterday and hung them at the cabin doorway to the cockpit. Dashed if a sea didn't souse the decks almost at once and make my poor pants far worse than before. We seemed to be getting nowhere and yet with considerable risk to gear.

In the morning I first hoisted a full mainsail. Next I set No. 2 jib. It blew up hard and I lowered and furled the main. Then after lunch I reefed the main fully and hoisted it again. Here I said, 'That's enough sail changing today. No more.' Handling that main in a blow takes some brawn and energy.

At 2000 hrs. the wind moderated and I logged that I ought to unreef the main and set the genoa . . . crazy loon! It was loud, wet going. Crashing through the smaller waves, swinging and slamming. We seemed to be going at at terrific pace but the cool-headed log said only 5¼ knots at the fastest. Then it blew up again and I changed down from No. 2 to No. 3 jib.

95

It was rather sport in the stem changing the sails, one second poised high up in the air looking down 20 feet to the sea – there was an overriding wave formation of about 15-foot seas – and the next with the stem at water level, as it were standing in the water.

At midnight I could not stand the bashing any longer, crashing through the seas; or the seas crashing into us. The sort of thing which is exciting and good sport in someone else's boat. I had noticed when changing jibs how ladylike and serene the yacht was with reefed mainsail only. I handed the jib and comparative peace followed. It is pressing on against the seas that makes most of the roughness. But it shows what a contribution is made by even a small jib. In ten hours with the mansail only we covered only 8¼ miles!

I couldn't sleep till three o'clock, overtired, but then got off till nine in the morning.

I started off afresh this morning with a fresh outlook. I refused to go on deck till I had had breakfast and even then would not set a jib till I had taken sextant shots of the sun before the extra bouncing started. It was still a Force 6 wind with the spray flying off horizontally and we have only been making 4 knots with No. 3 jib, and the main reefed. Nor are we going in the right direction. The wind is straight from New York.

It's like trying to reach a doorway with a man in it aiming a hose at you and the best you can do is to approach at an angle of 50° to the hose-stream one way or the other. Actually this port tack is now the worst but I will hold on till 1500 hrs. and try calling up a clipper on the R/T.

I rigged up the aerial afresh this morning, repairing it first. The lead in to the set had nearly parted from the aerial. Only one strand of wire left. Is that why I could not call anyone successfully? But already this morning I have tried several times to call any ship. I can hear nothing. Is it being in mid-Atlantic, or is there something wrong with the aerial still? I'm afraid Sheila will be worrying about me with no news for a fortnight. But I don't know what I can do about it.

Yesterday's run was the worst yet, 71½ miles and mostly in the wrong direction.

Goodbye my hopes of a fast passage. If only we were going east instead of west we should be making wonderful time with both wind and current favouring instead of opposing.

25th June. 0950 BST. It improved all day yesterday and by the evening, I was thinking what an incredible change it was from the night before. Sun shining, sea nearly calm, light air. I seized the opportunity to fill twelve bottles with paraffin from a two-gallon can. I even edged a pair of trousers and a sweater into the cockpit hoping they might dry. However, night fell before they had a chance to do that.

I tacked again to port tack as the wind backed and I left Miranda in charge with all sail set, ambling towards New York in the right direction at last, at 3 knots. I turned in and had a grand sleep from midnight till six o'clock, when I woke to find the wind had backed continually during the night and was now ESE., while we were headed south.

I trimmed the sails and Miranda to sail as nearly downwind as possible but this was 50° off the direction of New York. But I wanted the boat to do the best she could while I prepared our friends the twins.

Starting at 0700 hrs. (5 local time) I had the twin spinnakers set and drawing on our required course by 0915. This may seem slow to you for a mere sail change but to me it seemed quite a triumph. It was only the second time I had done it and much of the time was taken up doing things one should not have to do next time.

All the while on deck I am attached by a big web belt to a life-line. I promised Sheila I would do this. Someone very kindly presented me with a magnificent red and white lifebuoy but the trouble with that is that I should have to get back aboard somehow in order to throw myself the lifebuoy if I fell in.

A short length of rope is anchored half-way along the deck between cockpit and mast, one each side. I always use the weather one assuming I would fall downhill as it were. This I hook on to the belt and I use it for all work on the way to the mast. Of course it catches in everything on my way forward and again on my return aft. Also I frequently trip over it myself which adds to the gaiety if I'm in a tearing hurry to get back to the tiller.

The belt also has a short line with a hook of its own. With a bit of juggling I can hook this one to something at the mast so that I have a line behind my back to lean against if I want both hands at halliards or winch while the boat is lively or rolling heavily.

At the mast I transfer to another and shorter rope which tethers me when I go up to the stem to work the headsails on the forestays. Every trip back to the tiller from the stem means of course two transfers. And there are a lot of trips, not only to fetch gear but there is frequently a scamper to the tiller.

Each time a sail is dropped or hoisted the balance of pressure changes so much that the rudder must be reset quickly before the yacht overpowers the wind vane and ends in the chaos of a gybe or unwanted tack.

As regards the twins, I first prepared the small twin, hanked it onto the forestay and sheeted it loosely, halliard ready. Then I unlashed its spinnaker boom; topped this up to take its weight, fastened two down-guys to it to control its movement down, fore or aft, hooked one end into the grommet at the sail's clew and the other end into the gooseneck 7 feet up the mast. This spinnaker is now ready to hoist and the boom will be hoisted with it in place.

I fastened another down-guy to the twin goosenecks at the mast because they began creeping up the track on the mast last time due to the upward thrust of the two spinnaker booms. Next I made another of my *specialités de maison*, a rope strop slightly smaller to replace the one on the genoa's clew, which I dropped overboard while trying to fit it while the sail was set and drawing hard.

The next operation was to get rid of the mainsail. I half-lowered it, went back to the cockpit to harden the main boom in amidships to stop it from its lethal swinging as soon as the sail was completely down. Then finished lowering and furling it. Next I topped up Miranda so that her boom would not swing into the backstay when we turned downwind. Lastly I went through the same drill for the big genoa as for the smaller spinnaker. Hoisted it and returned

98

to the tiller to play with the tiller-lines and Miranda's tiller-lines until I was fairly hopeful that the boat would remain approximately on course, while I went forward to hoist No. 2 spinnaker.

I suppose that tiller adjustment also took a quarter of an hour. Once No. 2 was hoisted it was easy to set up the tiller-lines and Miranda for a steady course. Actually she is sailing 10° off course now two hours later, but that is nothing with such a set-up and is probably due to a wind change of that amount.

We are doing a nice, quiet, silky six knots. How delightful it is for a change after being days hard on the wind. I love the rumble of the bow-wave with a hint of distant thunder which you hear while peacefully running.

I called up time after time to try for contact with a ship yesterday. The set is perfectly all right. I suppose there just is no ship near or if there is it is not keeping a radio watch. I know these sets are only intended for a short range of 50 or 100 miles and it would be a bit of luck if one could contact a ship in mid-Atlantic with that range, let alone an aircraft.

To work! I must go and play with Miranda, her grip has definitely been slipping lately and once or twice caused me considerable embarrassment.

CHAPTER EIGHT

June 26th to 28th

Taking Miranda to Pieces – Big Following Seas –
Down Rig – Blowing Up Fast – Gale – Secure Every-
thing – Wind Increasing – Storm – Wind 80 m.p.h. –
Hurricane – Breakfast During Storm – Reading *The
Tempest* – The 'Sea Anchor' – Wind Reaches 100
m.p.h. – Unbelievable Noise – Twice Gybed – Wind
Abating to 80 m.p.h. – The Damage – Seas 25 Feet
High – Sheila Sails Today – Work on Miranda –
Swinging Like a Monkey – The Paraffin Patch –
Without Burgee – My Hat and Mildew – Explaining
the North Atlantic Current

26th June. 0900 hrs. or seven o'clock local time. All that
jaunty note yesterday morning that I have just caught sight
of was just gibberish. Although only a few hours it seems
so long ago that I have to make an effort to remember it.
I had Miranda topped up with only the little topsail working so that she could swing abaft the backstay.

She was linked to the tiller which was also prevented
from too much movement by shock-cord lines. I found this
arrangement had worked very well when the twin spinnakers were set the previous time and I had had no
need to link up the sheets from the outboard sail clews
direct to the tiller as the trade wind cruising yachts
always do.

I noticed by the tell-tale compass in the cabin and by the
sails clapping that the course was erratic and on going
above I found Miranda's clamp was slipping. I started
taking this to bits to try and cure the defect. But I never
succeeded because as soon as my back was turned to the
tiller the boat ran off one way or the other and the pistol-
like reports from the sail brought me back urgently. In a
few minutes I found I could not leave the tiller at all.

We were going at a great pace and the following seas would pick up the stern and slew it, bear it to one side or the other. The altered pressure on the sails would back up this movement and in a few seconds the boat would be coming round hard to wind with one spinnaker aback and big trouble ahead if the yaw was not checked at once.

I wondered what to do. Should I carry on at the helm for a few hours to take advantage of the 8 knots we were making in the right direction or should I take down the sail and rig up lines to the tiller according to trade-wind practice. Fortunately I got very sleepy and could hardly keep my eyes open. So I decided to down the rig.

You will have realized that the wind had been increasing very fast, but, preoccupied with steering and thinking what to do with the rig, I had not paid attention to it. I realized it quick enough by the time I came to hand the big genoa. First I slacked off the sheet to let the pole forward and decrease the area of sail offering to the wind. The bellied-out sail flapped madly, and when I slacked away the halliard so that the sail was partly down the stay, the noise was terrific and the boat began slewing wildly to come up to wind with the genoa's big flapping belly behind the other sail. I rushed back and corrected the course then back to the genoa. I managed to gather some of it and pass a sail tie round. Then slacked more halliard to let the lower half of the sail into the water which I correctly assumed would keep that part quiet while I dealt with the 14-foot pole.

I got the sail down in the end, but had to use some strong-arm tactics. The fact is the wind was increasing fast as I worked. I had more trouble with the smaller sail. When I let the boom forward, the end holding the clew of the sail was about six feet outboard of the foredeck. I got a length of rope round the middle of the sail but the part between the deck and the boom began gyrating madly. At last I got this under control by twisting the sail round and round at the deck until the loose area was whittled down and I could secure it with a sail tie.

By now there was a gale blowing and I had only just got the sails down in time. I thought at one stage that the genoa was going to blow itself to pieces. It was 1045 when

I had gone on deck to fix Miranda; it was 1600, 5¼ hours later that I got below again.

I had a big blow on my hands and I worked hard to secure everything. I was pretty relieved at the start to get the spinnaker poles down to the deck and lashed down. Next came Miranda, who had begun to break up. Her topping lift had stranded and parted letting the spanker drop and one of the halliards of the little topsail had done the same.

First I got the spanker off and topped up its boom by passing a sail tie round to secure it to the gaff. I had a lot of trouble to get the topsail off; the soaking wet coils of halliard were jammed tight. I had to work with hands at full stretch above my head while balancing like a monkey standing on the pulpit.

It would have been easy to get fussed; it was now blowing great guns and Miranda's 14-foot mast I was working at was free to swing with the wind, while I was tangled up in all its stays while working on it. I thought of the old wind-jammers where they had to treat a gale as an everyday matter and very likely had iced ropes to handle. There seemed fifty jobs to do, but I did them all. Such as lowering the mainsail boom to the deck and lashing it down.

1330 hrs. It was only when I finished my toils that I realized what was going on. The din was appalling, a high-pitch screech or scream dominating. Plenty of spray peppering everything and seas hitting periodically with a bonk! Crash! The wind was 80 m.p.h., that makes about 70 knots. I always think of high wind speeds in m.p.h. because I measure them by the slipstream of a light plane which I was well used to.

An hour later I realized the boat was lying on the unfavourable tack headed ese., beam-on to the wind from nne. I thought this a pity to be headed away from my destination so dressed up again and coaxed the boat round in a gybe to the opposite tack using full rudder to get her round. She was going pretty fast broadside-on to the wind, at 3 knots I judged, and I tried to induce her to lie more nearly head to wind but she absolutely refused anything except broadside-on wherever the tiller was set. The wind I assessed now at 90 m.p.h. I went below and had a good breakfast of my usual fry-up of potatoes, onions and three eggs. I then went to sleep reading *The Tempest*.

At 2030 hrs. I donned my wet kit again and tried to slow the boat down. She seemed to be getting an awful bashing from the seas. I got out a big motor tyre and shackled it onto the anchor chain, paying out 10 fathoms of this, which is ⁵⁄₁₆-inch link, over the stern. I also paid out 20 fathoms of 2½-inch warp over the stern.

I filled a tin with oil and, puncturing the tin, hung it over the side amidships in a piece of canvas. I concluded it was not the slightest use, the engine oil was too thick and we were moving too fast. The anchor chain left a white wake as it cut through the water at about 3 knots. I put the wind now at 100 m.p.h.

The noise was unbelievable and made me wonder how anything could stand up to the wind. However, I informed my ignorant self quite sharply that that was nonsense. What about the chaps climbing Everest, what was a 90- or 100-mile wind to them?

At 2200 I worked out that we were headed into the eye of the storm. I dressed very reluctantly and climbed out with difficulty into the cockpit. I found I had a dry mouth when I started to do anything, but felt better when I did it.

With full rudder held on with some strength she slowly gybed round. She seemed to take the seas a shade easier on this tack.

I couldn't help laughing when I went below again. All the same books, cushions, clothes back all over the floor and the same papers. I kept on gathering things up but after every manœuvre there they all were back again.

I dozed but could not sleep. Waiting for the next comber made me tense. I have not been in a wind like this at sea since I was in a typhoon on the China Sea – in a steamer. It seemed impossible that a small boat could survive. Of course it sounds much worse below, especially the seas landing on top of the cabin.

I found I could see the spinnaker poles with a torch through the cabin ports and was relieved to find them both still lashed down. I dreaded having to chase around after one of these to secure it in the dark. Reason told me that far less-strong boats than this survived such storms.

I realized as soon as I got below that I had made a bad blunder in working out that the SE. tack would take me away from the storm centre. The other NW. one would. But the boat seemed better off on this tack and I let it ride. After all, I wanted a boat after the storm; what did a few miles away from New York matter?

But at 0400 hrs. (two o'clock local time) I could not bear being on the wrong tack any longer, got up and changed over. The gear seemed intact as far as I could see except for some of the dodger lashings which had parted. How those dodgers stand up to it is a miracle. Some seas were breaking right over the boat. One filled the patent ventilator and shot a jet into the cabin, but everything there was wet already.

I brought in Old Faithful, the riding light, filled and lit it and rigged it in the stern as usual. It seemed completely unperturbed. An amazing lamp. Another amazing thing is the Aladdin wick-stove which I have had going all the storm. A great comfort with everything wet. It doesn't seem to care a damn.

The heel indicator registers up to 55° and I see it come up against the stop while it is difficult to stand up or move about the cabin; but Aladdin cares for none of these things. The wind had abated, and I estimated it at only 80 m.p.h. I expect big seas later and it is those which count.

We jogged along towing the sea anchor and warp at about 2–3 knots all night, right on course.

At eleven o'clock in the morning I emerged once more to survey the scene. The wind had dropped but was a good Force 8 or 9 as I was well aware when I climbed on the stern pulpit to make temporary repairs to Miranda. It was only seeing her spanker boom caught up in the backstay which brought me out of my hermit's cabin. I lashed the spanker to the gaff as far up as I could reach standing on the pulpit and working with one hand stretched fully up. The gaff gooseneck bolt has gone which may cause me some trouble.

The only damage other than to Miranda that I could find was a life rail stanchion anchoring a dodger which had been torn loose where bolted to the bulwark . . . wonderful! (Later I found that actually five stanchions had the

104

bolts fastening them to the bulwark snapped and one had carried away part of the fairly heavy bulwark.)

I pumped 117 strokes, due to an after-peak hatch being open. I suppose it must have been sucked open by a sea coming aboard. I was astonished not to find a lot more water as a result and concluded it had not been open for long.

The wind was NNE. The seas were turbulent, very impressive like mountainous country modelled in white-capped water. There were no regular waves. Looking down from a crest to the trough below I judged the height to be 25 feet. Now the wind is so much less, I can often hear a 'striker' sea coming. There is a lull in the wind, presumably when we are deep in the trough, then the boat mounts sideways and I can hear a sizzling from the comber. If it does not strike the boat the boat seems to shoot over the crest and land a heavy belly-whopper in the trough below.

I wonder if a storm jib set aback would ease this deadly rolling. It is quite dangerous trying to move in the cabin; it is very difficult not to get caught off balance and thrown across. I must start thinking how to mend Miranda.

I hope those other poor devils have not been caught in this. I'm sure it would be much worse in a smaller boat. But one might be only 200 miles away and completely miss an intense little storm like this.

Personally I am fagged to the bone. A cup of tea may infuse a bit of tannin to my jaded spirit.

Sheila is due to sail today; I say she won't be put off by lack of news and the bad weather if she hears of it. She is one of spirit and not to be deterred.

Poor old Miranda, she looks like a knitting-bag which the cat has got loose in, with fag-ends of cordage and parted halliards flying loose . . . the sail tie flapping like chocolate-box ribbon, otherwise a forlorn skeleton.

2045 hrs. BST. Whacko! I thought we had settled down to a new start. It seemed so calm, when, just as I started to write, a sea broke over the whole boat. We had made a modest fresh start by 1915 hrs. when I had No. 3 jib set and drawing — no mainsail. It is still blowing pretty hard, Force 6. I have trimmed the rudder so that she is keeping herself more or less on course.

Miranda is out of action and even if it fell to light airs I wouldn't set a mainsail tonight. Miranda is my first consideration, she needs brains to put her right again and I can't afford to tire myself popping up every few minutes during the night to retrim a main and jib. With jib only I think she will amble along all night.

A good job you can't smell what's going on in the mid-Atlantic; I'm having my favourite *aperitif*, gruyere cheese and garlic, lashings of it. But I am being driven crazy by the rolling. I put one foot on the chart table to steady up while I cleaned the potatoes; the boat promptly rolled with a snap right over the other way and the saucepanful of water and potatoes went over the cabin sole.

I should be really in the soup without Miranda – so I did some preliminary work on her before setting the jib.

I unrigged the spanker boom completely. Then I fitted a bolt to the gaff gooseneck to replace the one lost. (Oh, God! this rolling; it is a wonder it doesn't break one's neck, it is so snappy.) I removed the stranded and parted halliards and studied how to replace the one out at the end of the gaff for the topsail. The only way to reach the sheave 14 feet above the deck, was to stand on the end of the topped-up main boom and that really needs some calm. However, I hope to devise some way round the difficulty during the night. The same problem with the sheave . . .

27th June. The above seems to have petered out. Something called me out I suppose. Today has been a very nice change of weather. Sun and calm. Racing yachtsmen may take umbrage at my welcoming a calm but I loved it. Especially as I had to repair Miranda before proceeding; pretty well a whole day's work. I only hope my rivals have had the same delightful calm themselves for a day; I wish them weeks of calm!!

It is a great pleasure from where I am sitting here tonight to be able to watch Miranda back on the job again and the ship ambling along with that queer wobble of her stern and the water guggling along the hull.

Miranda needed some attention. I started at 0900 hrs. BST and have only knocked off for dinner, which I have just finished at 2325 hrs., 14½ hours later. I won't go into

106

details, she needed a lot – new halliards, a topping lift etc. The fact that I have been on the job all day, gives an idea.

The rolling was really nasty snap-back stuff – it was very difficult to stand on the deck and even sitting on it, one was slid suddenly from one side to the other. There was one hilarious scene which must have made the fishes laugh – Miranda is 14 feet tall from the deck and very slender with it. I wanted to reach the top to reeve the new topping lift. I climbed up in my best monkey style. You know how Miranda works, the vane sails make the whole mast rotate in its socket or sleeve and two arms at the bottom or foot have lines which pull the tiller one way or another according to how the vane weathercocks.

I should add that the rolling has been really maddening, due to the sea left by the storm. As soon as I got up aloft the first roll swung the whole thing round 180° due to my weight. I hung on pretty tight. I waited for it to come back; instead, the roll back sent me right round. The next roll occurred just right and spun me again and in about 15 seconds. I was spinning round like a scared dormouse clinging to a spinning top.

As a matter of fact I wasn't worried about myself, after my first astonishment. I only regretted I couldn't see it because I thought it must look the most comical turn. But I was scared stiff for Miranda. She was not built and stressed for a load like this. If her mast snapped, it might take me a week to repair it. I got out of my perch as soon as I could, having to catch the pulpit with a leg dropped down as I spun round.

Another silly thing occurred ... I was cleaning Miranda's clamp, after refitting it, with paraffin and spilt some on the rubberized deck. This gave me unbelievable trouble; it made the deck so slippery that I just could not stand on the deck in my deck boots. This was maddening, because I wanted to work on that exact spot all day. I washed it with soap solution and water. Then I tried a French detergent with more water. Then I sluiced it with several buckets of water but none of this made the slightest difference. I just could not stand on it. Finally I took my boots off and worked in bare feet.

It's nice to be on our way again, even if only with a

modest little breeze. That storm cost me more than two whole days. But perhaps I should not grumble, no, it is just as nice to be a starter again.

I now find that four stanchions had their through-bolts snapped, one or two others have their angle pieces bent and the fastening started. I guess I was lucky to get off so lightly.

I can't find another burgee to replace the one blown to bits, with nothing left of it. The odd thing is that a pair of underpants which I had optimistically put out to dry on the cabin top, securing them by buttoning them round a handrail, were still there next morning quite undamaged. (They still are because the drying time today was not long enough to dry them out.)

I do wish I knew if my rivals got caught by that storm and if so how they got on. I believe it was only a small diameter tornado type perhaps only 100 miles wide and another boat quite near could be having a nice fine day.

I took two sun sights today but have been too busy to work them out. They are there in case I don't get any more. A nasty wind, a dense bank of fog came up this afternoon and I began shutting the hatches and taking things below but after dropping two huge raindrops on me the fog bank cleared off again.

I don't know how far we sailed last night, I haven't worked it out. I was determined to get a good sleep. I knew we could be going twice as fast with more sail, but I felt tired right through. I am sure I was right to get a rest and start afresh rather than struggle for the extra few knots at the price of remaining tired.

I had a good lesson today in how much time a clear head can save. I had been trying to get a block to the peak of Miranda's gaff to replace the halliard there which carried away. It is impossible to reach it, even by climbing the mast. I tried for about an hour to drop a strop with a block attached over the top of the gaff using a boathook. The boathook is 12 feet long and substantial. With the mad rolling and being unable to stand on the most needed patch of deck, I began to take a very poor view of the whole enterprise. I retired for lunch (a very substantial one) and another idea turned up without the least pang.

108

I made two loops about 18 inches apart at the end of a length of rope and attached a weight to the end loop. I stuck the boathook in the other loop and dropped the weighted loop over the gaff collecting it the other side with the boathook and bringing it down. It was so easy that I felt a dolt to have spent so long so angrily trying the other way.

Time to turn in. Oh, I'll have a look to see what we did do last night – 29 miles, not to be sniffed at ambling along with only No. 3 jib, so as to give its owner a big zizz.

28th June. 0515 hrs. Miranda got me out of my cosy berth at 0315 hrs. The course had deteriorated to 240° and the boat was beginning to make heavy weather of it. How I hate that change from good sleep to nasty toil.

It was a black night with a heavy drizzle turning into rain now and then. It was my fault, not Miranda's. She had slipped again but when I took over I spent ¾ hour working hard to try and trim. As soon as the boat came up or ran off 30° she developed a really tough weather or lee helm as the case might be. This occurred at the point where the vane arms have least leverage, just when most was needed. In the end I found – I suppose you will laugh, it will seem so simple and obvious to you – that both main and genoa were sheeted in much too hard for a broad reach. When I freed them appropriately the helm became quite docile. Miranda has had no trouble with it since.

I feel depressed. At 1000 hrs. today I shall be 17 days out and will be lucky if I find we are half-way. (I have not worked up a position for several days; must try to find time today.) To crack a 30-day passage would need 1,500 miles in 13 days, an average of 116 per day which I fear is too much for me. The time and effort lost in frequent sail-changing slows me up. A big boat like this (for single-handed work) pays off with steady weather. Otherwise I reckon the small boat with its small sails has the advantage.

I considered one gale must be allowed for but I've had the luck to strike more than the average. I remember how Robert Clark, describing a race across the Atlantic in *Joliette*, Freddy Morgan's boat of Robert's design about the same size as *Gipsy Moth*, said they only reefed three times, once in anticipation of a squall which did not arrive. And I think he had his genoa set for 85% of the time. Of course I know that is going the other way – west to east when the prevailing wind and current are both with you. I'm just trying to make my point of how much you need luck for a fast race.

0540 hrs. Still as black as pitch; I suppose dawn won't be till 0615 or 0630 in this longitude.

Thank you for letting me air my little moan. I'll try for another packet of sleep. I really ought to begin sleeping more by day because I expect I shall have to be on watch all night in us coastal waters.

I wish I could think up a way of getting a time signal. I haven't had one for days. I can't hear any British stations and none of the wwv wavelengths are on my R/T set or Heron-homer set. I must start listening to usa broadcasts at random but if there is a special time-giving station (wwv is the Bureau of Standards) which sends out time signals continually on about twelve different wavelengths why should any broadcasting station do the same? Who could imagine an old navigator like me could be such a dolt as to be caught without means of getting one of the wavelengths of wwv?

I'll manage. I can always get a latitude at noon and will just have to run down it in old sailing whaler style. Only of course you do really need a look-out to make a proper job of that method.

1700 BST. Woe is with us once again. While some of us suck the savours of delight eating Danish blue cheese on gingernuts – a very advanced taste this, reached by few as yet – woe is waiting round the corner. My hat, the most comfortable of the type, be it Homburg or Stetson, I have ever had, personally selected for me by the proprietor of one of the world's best hat-shops (Scotts of Piccadilly) . . . words fail me till I have made the tea. Ah, that's better . . . well, I specially placed a hook for this hat in the safest snuggest place I could think of: just round behind the bulkhead of the forepeak. I thought it was the one place where nothing could crush it. Just now I looked at it to find it covered with mildew.

I take a gloomy view of everything today. Grey seas, grey skies, fog, drizzle.

I spent a good part of the morning bringing my navigation up to date. It *is* a fascinating art or craft, I suppose for the same reason that detective stories fascinate otherwise reasonable people. Finding the clues and deducing a certainty out of a lot of possibilities, probabilities or even improbabilities. You can't be sure of any of the information you get, yet you solve the problem by deductive intuition.

This morning I worked up my dead reckoning from the 19th to yesterday the 27th. I allowed for the speed we were moving forward when broadside on to the hurricane – strength of wind and the amount we were being pushed sideways through the water by that wind at the same time. This may sound rather a puff of boloney but it was quite easy really – I merely noted the angle which the anchor chain of my sea anchor was making with the fore-aft line of the ship.

This DR is quite a job really . . . for instance on the day of the 24th–25th June there were fourteen changes of course logged with the distance sailed on each course. Each course has to have the appropriate correction for magnetic variation which is 24° here and compass deviation which is another 4° on those headings.

For easy plotting I had a fine instrument (I think it was a war-time issue to Coastal Command) which is simply a transparent sheet with the compass degrees around the edge which rotates over a piece of squared paper. One can plot the 14 courses and distances on this in a minute or two. Unfortunately it shot across the cabin in the hurly-burly and was smashed but a piece of it survived big enough for me to get my answers with a bit of mental jugglery.

Then I worked out the two sun shots I got yesterday. The result? The sun fix was 98 miles east (080°/98 miles to be exact) of the DR position. This was a bit of a shaker at first glance and I was preparing to be more gloomy when I remembered the North Atlantic current, the continuation of the Gulf Stream. I studied the US hydrographic chart for June and found it recorded that the current flows east at

0·4 of a knot in one part of the area I was working in and ½ knot in the other half. Splitting the difference at ·45 of a knot over the whole area, eight days of this works out at 8 days × 24 hours × ·45 knots = 86·4 miles. This reduced the discrepancy to a tolerable figure and I was less wreathed in gloom. (I must go and tack; the wind has backed.)

9 Old Faithful didn't mind what the weather was like

This was in rough weather too, trysail set, but it looks a flat calm

10   They were rougher than they look

CHAPTER NINE

June 29th to July 2nd

Fine Day – The *Mauretania* – Unable to Signal –
Nearing the Grand Banks – Indigo Blue Sea – Squalls
and Splashes – Fathers' Day in Mid-Atlantic – The
Five Loaves – In the Gulf Stream – Barometer and
Braces – High Jinks in the Night – The Giant Shadow
– Listening to Canada – No Ice Reports – Sailing
Again after Gale – Loss of the Thermos – The Pleasure
of Overcoming Difficulties

29th June. 1145 BST. It is fine today – so far – I'm sitting
in the cockpit with my tankard of Guinness to hand. The
cabin looks like chaos cubed but I felt I must stop for a
while or I'd go round the bend.

Yesterday I never got back to my blue book and red pen.
It was just one thing after the other. Here is the bare bones
of it. Changed tack 1800 hrs. Rain, nasty weather, wind
steadily increasing. 1900 changed from genoa to No. 2 jib
and the ship sailed faster because there had been too much
wind for the big sail. 2000 hrs. finished fully reefing the
mainsail. Fed-up. No more sail changes tonight. If forced
I will hand the existing ones but nothing else is to go up
before dawn.

Worried about poor Miranda's stays, they are so loose.
What has she been up to, poor gal? She is flogging about
much too much in this blast of air coming approximately
direct from New York. I refastened most of her stays for
her by use of lanyards.

At 2050 hrs. the *Mauretania* passed looking very solid
and rather majestic in the dirty grey weather. I rushed for
my Aldis lamp to signal and ask to be reported. Hell! the
electrics are fused. No masthead light to signal with either.
I looked at my hand-torch but it was laughable to think of

113

a ship seeing it from a mile away. I tried Morse with a tea-towel but the wind made that into a joke. It is not decreed, I believe, that I should send a message.

She sounded off with three blasts of her foghorn and was on her way, leaving me a trifle forlorn. I must have looked like a shipwrecked character drawn by Thurber waving that tea-towel. No one could have deduced I was trying to signal. I relied on the Aldis lamp and had no hoist of flags ready (MIK), asking to be reported to Lloyds. I was left behind to horrible grey skies and every look of another gale. Don't they have any fine weather in this hemisphere?

Ah! Noon! Day's run. Log reads 1632, making a day's run of 104 miles. Now becalmed. I must lower mainsail, which is doing itself no good slatting, and interferes with my Guinness enjoyment. I thought I had better snap the sun with the sextant at the same time in case it gets clouded over later. We are slowly nearing the Grand Banks and could easily not have a sight of the sun for a fortnight because of fog.

After *Mauretania* left me to my blues among all the greys, I tried to call her up on the R/T, but no luck.

I cooked the dinner and was just starting to eat it when the wind veered to put us on a northerly course. I couldn't enjoy my fried cod's roe with accessories if we were sailing at right angles to the direction of New York. So I left the feast, dressed again in full kit of rainwear and tacked ship.

The weather looked horrible with those beastly dreaded black standing squalls here and there. This was at 2235 hrs. BST. and soon after midnight I turned in for a miserable night. *Gipsy Moth* had one of her pig-jumping bouts. I suppose she's young, only launched last September and must have her fling, slinging her weight about. It was one of those nasty short seas like you get off the east coast of England.

Gipsy M. would prance up to a sea and pig-jump it. This caused me to take off from my berth for an instant. Then she'd land, slam! on the other side of the wave which meant for me thumping back on the bunk. She would vary this by twisting on the way up the wave which made my wretched body roll hard against one side of the berth or the other. Add to this the whine of the wind in the rigging and the flogging of the jib leech in extra strong gusts and you have the finest ingredients for a good night's unrest.

I got up once at 0120 for a squall, saying, half-asleep, that I must hand the mainsail. Then I thought, no, with this reduced rig the spars would stand a gale easily, and if the No. 2 jib blows itself out it is the only sail among my suit of sails which I really cannot grow fond of. As far as I am concerned it can blow itself to hell. With which conclusion I reblanketed myself.

Miranda kept the ship headed west for 8½ hours while I loafed among the blankets and I got up at 8.30 to find the sun shining but squalls still about. During the night *Gipsy M*. had done 37 miles in 8½ hours – 4⅓ knots, which is as good as I could hope for in a slamming sea, hard on the wind, in squally conditions, with the main fully reefed and the owner below. (The sea has that deep indigo blue today which is so attractive.)

As soon as I got up this morning I decided to time my headsail changes and unreefing. I fancy this is where my Viking black-bearded rival will gain on me. It is a major operation for me to change headsails, or reef, and the ship almost stands still as soon as the headsail is lowered.

In my last yacht *Gipsy Moth II*, an 8-tonner, it only took me about a quarter of the time to reef as it does for this 13-tonner. I admit I aim for a better reefed sail now. This one sets beautifully when I have reefed it using my arrangement of tackle and shock-cord to haul the leech out tight.

Pity the poor yachtsman. At every sail change or trim, if racing, he has to achieve an ideal aerofoil, that is, make the sail take the shape of one, which eluded the greatest scientists and mathematicians from the time of Leonardo da Vinci, till that of de Havilland or thereabouts.

Changing No. 2 jib to genoa, including change of sheet lead and rigging a preventer on the mainsail boom, also trimming the sail and Miranda to get on course afterwards, took 19 minutes starting from the cabin sole.

Unreefing the main took me 21 minutes but I had some bad management to contend with during the operation. After getting the main hoisted I found the top batten was foul of the R/T aerial so I had to lower the sail, slack away the R/T halliard and then make them both up again. Of course this was in nice conditions. Any fool can set the sail, it's taking it off which needs the seaman.

30th June. 1300 hrs. BST (or about 2 hours 40 minutes earlier local time). I'm somewhat diffident about this drop into the ordinary humdrum of life, but I must admit that when I awoke at 1100 hrs. this morning I was exhausted. Perhaps I should have had a cup of coffee or something before going on deck, but I hate to neglect good sailing-wind which I could hear it was.

I had trouble in getting the main hoisted. I just had run out of sheer muscle-power. Of course I made it much worse by letting the ship come about during the operation, with resultant chaos, jib aback, sheets flogging, mainboom hard up against the standing runner and so on and so forth. Don't all we yachtsmen know it? But you would think I ought to be able to avoid it after these weeks of handling the ship.

I do miss having no burgee or racing-flag or anything at the masthead. With one's head down messing about with halliards, winch and cleats at the mast it is difficult to be aware all the time of where the wind is, to know if the ship is turning etc. I'm used to glancing at the burgee aloft every now and then to check that all is right. Not only was the burgee blown to bits and then stripped off its wire hoist but the flag halliard parted when I came to lower the burgee stick and the stick disappeared.

Eventually I got the main up except for a baggy pocket at the foot of the luff. John Illingworth, one of the world's two leading ocean racers with Carlton Mitchell, would never let such a thing happen. I only wish John could take over for a day and put everything right for me.

I decided to get my breakfast and try for the last few inches of hoist thereafter. But it will not be for some time because I am moving slowly today. My first cup of coffee I stupidly upset. (One more cup and then I'll really call a committee meeting to see whether it is time to start the toil again.)

What's so depressing is that all this exhaustion talk stems from the efforts made to get almost nowhere. Tack, tack,

tack; north-west gradually headed to north, tack to sw. but almost never able to head for New York, wsw. For every 100 miles sailed NW. or SW. I only approach New York by 70 miles; in fact, don't even do that because the adverse Atlantic current is all the time carrying us back along our course from England at approximately ten miles a day.

Even if headed direct for New York at 5 knots one must sail two hours out of every twenty-four hours simply to counter the current. But if the wind is from the New York direction and one can only head within 45° of it one side or the other it requires three hours' sailing every day simply to counter the current. In the last five days to yesterday, thanks to the storms, squalls, gales and adverse winds and to the owner going asleep we have only advanced 190 miles along our route. We'll probably arrive in 1961 at that rate. Our heading at the moment 240° compass is 45° off the required course of 285°.

Last night was even more disastrous from a racing point of view, than usual. At midnight I decided we were carrying too much sail, so changed from genoa to No. 2 jib and lowered and furled the main. Handling that main in the dark and in a disturbed sea is really a job for Hercules or my black-bearded Viking friend rather than for me, especially the boom.

While hanging on to it to tie the furled sail to it and it swings from port to starboard due to a snap-over roll, the blow in the chest when it comes up against the end of its swing is a real grunt-maker. I hated cutting down the sail area but I was proved right when a gale-strength squall hit us in the middle of the night. I was aroused with a terrific crash . . . a clash of crockery, etc. and water in my face where I lay on the settee berth.

In the dark I wondered whatever had happened. When I found out, the only thing to do was laugh. I had a bucket hanging from a hook under a cabin port the other side of the cabin from where I was lying. It was catching the water from a biggish leak there and I emptied it about once a day. When heeled at 40° it was nearly over my head. *Gipsy Moth*, while so heeled had taken one of her famous Bechers Brook jumps over a big wave and what could be more effective than a bucket of water with a few cups and

117

glasses added for sound effects, landing in one's face while asleep?

I found the course had crept round to north so I dressed in oilskins and tacked. The squall died down while I was up and I had a lot of trouble to get trimmed without Miranda. I did not want her engaged for the rest of the night for fear of her getting damaged in more storm-squalls.

In a short clearing in the sky I saw the new moon on her back. Thank heaven, we shall have some worthwhile moon-light in a few days' time. There were a lot of combers about and when the wind dropped in a lull I was surprised how long I could hear them coming with a steady hiss, not very loud before they struck the ship.

Several times after I got back to my berth I turned out again to try and trim. *Gipsy M.* began turning in complete circles and after listening to four of these, waiting each time she came back to 240° on the compass, to see if she was going round again or going to settle, I finally had to get up again. I was so fed up with the beastly dressing and undressing in clammy wet oilskins and sea-boots that I went out in a shirt and underpants only. But later I won-dered if that was wise straight from warm blankets. How-ever, my hurt chest seems better, which is wonderful news for me and really nothing else matters by comparison.

Well, once more into the breeches, dear friends, once more, to continue delaying our arrival in New York by end-less dodging of the contrary blast therefrom.

I have made medical history: every joint this morning is made of malleable lead.

I forgot to say why last night was more disastrous; under the jib only the ship will not point within 45° of the wind, but more like 70° so that all my loss of sleep, loss of good sailing wind, while asleep this morning and general sap-ping of my moral marrow fat is simply in order to keep the ship headed no worse than 220° compass which amounts to nearly due south (true direction) when New York lies at nearly west.

Finally, thank you for listening to my moans, you have done me a power of good.

1735 hrs. Gone dreary despair and dull cares. I decided

this was Father's Day in mid-Atlantic. No more sail-changing today or press-on nonsense of that sort. First I retired to the Hammam, making sure the door would not slam unexpectedly on my person and had a good fresh-water bath. This is a bold way of describing a wash all over with flannel, water and soap.

I can assure you it was a most acrobatic ablution with the ship at her usual bucking tricks. After that a shave which saw the death of a new razor blade. Then, oh! luxury! a clean set of clothes. Oh, yes, I can see your lips curling in a sneer only suppressed through your gentlemanly instincts, but clean clothes are not too easy on a jaunt like this. Either you must make your stock last as long as the voyage which may require quite a number of changes, or else you must start a laundry. So far I have not had the time to spare for the latter. In any case I still have not got dry the pair of Dr Deimel's underwear which I put out hopefully about June 17th. So if it takes more than eighteen days to dry one pair of pants I think a laundry might be rather exasperating.

Then I opened up the sacks of potatoes and onions in the forepeak, both saturated in seawater like my hat there. After opening up the potato sack I feel I ought to have some nice new potatoes to eat by the time I reach New York.

I also fished out all my remaining loaves, cut off the mildew which meant a slice up to half an inch thick off every side of the loaf. The five loaves remaining are now in my portable oven on the Primus having a second baking. Whether this is a success I will tell you later. If not, I must bake afresh, but this does require a lot of attention over quite a long period. Perhaps the next weather prank will be a calm for a week in which case baking will be one of the first chores.

Next I sat down to a very satisfying lunch of Chinook salmon with new potatoes and some onion followed by Danish blue cheese. Setting genoa and all that racing nonsense is off La Carte for today; I feel I would purr if I could after my lunch, without a care.

Looking back, it is odd why I should have been so uneasy and unhappy last night. I suppose I expected the squall we had and it would have been very embarrassing in the middle of the night with a full suit of sails set.

1st July. 0040 hrs. I shall have to get a move on as this seems to be my last blue book left to write in. I have just come in after finishing my deck work, tidying up to see that all the running parts of halliards are clear, the dinghy lashings in good order, rigging the riding lamp, etc. Then I tacked to port tack again and hope I am right.

My BC (best course) is now 280° on the compass (which is 265° true). I was getting down to 225° compass on the starboard tack, and am now on 335° on the other. Sometimes heading better but that is a fair assessment; the seas keep on casting the ship's head off and if I keep her hard on the wind under Miranda's control, the seas slow her up too much. Both tacks are equally bad at the moment, but the point is which way will the wind go? I think it will back to the SW. from west where it is now. If I'm right I'll have, I hope, a peaceful night; if not, I'll have to tack again.

The seas seem much nastier on this tack, I can't understand why, because I had a good look before tacking and they were coming exactly downwind and therefore should be the same for *Gipsy M.* on either tack. The seawater is warm and this combined with the muggy overcast weather and nasty squalls I take to indicate we are in Gulf Stream water. I think the deep clear blue is another sign.

Why all this nastiness? I say; why can't it mix more with our chilly northern water without endless squalling and turbulence? With all its natural gifts coming from the West Indies one would like it to be benign, gracious and calm as well as warm. Just imagine if one had a teeny-weeny part of it welling up on the south coast of England. That lovely warm tropical sea bathing. I'll turn in but fear this W. Indian water means another bumpy night.

Sad PS. I dropped my barometer tonight and bust it; an old friend which has been with me on all my flights starting in 1929 and all my sea voyages and races.

Happy PS. I made myself a pair of braces for my oilskin deck-pants with enormous success. These trousers always worked their way down however hard I belted them up.

The number of times those damn things have hindered, hampered and harassed me by beginning to slip just as I got into a tizzie on the foredeck in the dark and wet! It is another of those music-hall chestnuts which are based on personal tragedy.

1500 hrs. (1200 local time.) Is it still only July 1st? It seems days ago since it started at midnight. I did get to sleep about half-past one but at 0230 I was woken by a thunderous crash of a sea on board, got up, dressed in oilies and went on deck to see if anything serious had happened. Not a thing visible out of place, not to say smashed. I was astonished. However from then on it was high jinks for the rest of the night.

First I found we were only doing 2·8 knots which was all wrong. Try as I would I could not trim her. Of course, the reason is probably quite plain to you as it is to me now, but either I was stupid when roused from sleep or I have been getting more used to high winds. She was being over-powered by the wind and refusing to move. At 0300 hrs. I decided to tack; the other tack was of equal value, the wind, as usual, being right in the eye looking in the direction of New York. I thought the ship went better, with less crashing about on the starboard tack.

At last I realized I had a strong wind on my hands, that it was already Force 7, and increasing. I tried to reef the main. I had trouble to turn the handle which operates the worm and pinion gear. I did not like to use the strong arm because of the breakages of the same gear on other boats which I knew had occurred through forcing it.

I started checking the main sheet to pay off the main boom. As soon as I relieved the wind pressure on the mainsail the ship fairly shot into the night like a scalded cat. I thought that if I let all the wind out of it, I must be able to roll the boom easily. We went faster than ever.

It really was sport, exhilarating, tearing through the black night with the bow-waves boiling white in the light of Tilley hanging in the stern. I went on paying off the boom until the whole mainsail was just flat and undulating. We just went faster still. I would say we were doing 10 knots.

When I went forward to the mast I saw a fantastic sight.

121

A huge black giant in the sky ahead – most eerie – as if I had rubbed Aladdin's lamp and its Djinn or Genie had appeared from nowhere. The truth was we had sailed into a patch of light fog and the powerful white light from Tilley in the stern had cast my huge shadow onto the fog-patch ahead as I walked up the deck to the mast.

Finally I realized I just could not handle reefing with the sail set without undue risk to the reefing gear so I lowered the whole sail and gathered the madly slatting mess of sail by armfuls out of the night and tied it a little at a time to subdue it. We were still going about 5 knots with only No. 2 jib set, so I put the mainsail out of mind for the night.

I finally got back to sleep about eight in the morning and slept till eleven but it isn't enough and I'm exhausted again today.

The truth is that I have badly boobed in my expectations for this race. I never expected to have to change sails every hour or so much of the time. I thought the wind would hold steady out in the ocean for days at a time and that the chief drawback with a big boat was the difficulty of hand-ling the sails if caught in a squall. No, I never anticipated this sail changing every hour or two.

2230 hrs. BST. If this wouldn't give you the willies, whatever would? Rain, fog, gale squalls, capricious, nasty and very forceful seas, grey skies, grey seas with white horses. Everything wet. And then people have the nerve to run down British Isles weather. I wouldn't mind, I think, if we could only go straight to our objective but as usual all day we have not been able to head closer than 50° from where I want to go.

In one way it is rather amazing to achieve 50° with only a jib set. Well, it is nothing to complain of compared with Slocum's sailing through the Magellan Strait, for two months held up by incessant gales from where he wanted to head. On the other hand he was not racing and racing makes one impatient.

I wonder if you can read this? You must be a wizard if you can. This reminds me of when I used to be immensely proud that I could roll a cigarette with one hand while cantering (in New Zealand, where they never used to gallop or trot their horses in the back country). But that is

122

not much more difficult than writing in a bucking, pig-jumping, twisting bronco of a yacht.

We are under jib only because a sudden gale-force squall made me lower the main and it has stayed down since. We are averaging 4½ knots with the jib and I reckon it is not worth trying to get another half a knot or possibly a knot by setting a trysail considering the immense effort involved. Effort is in short supply and tonight owes me a sleep.

I have one bit of good news. A Canadian station on my R/T set. It was a surprise after the silence of the mid-Atlantic. It was CBC – St John's, Newfoundland, and I got a sort of time signal, thank goodness. The announcer said 'It will be so and so in five seconds' time', and I took his word for it. According to that my watch is 28 seconds out which means that my sextant sight yesterday puts us 7' of longitude farther west than I had calculated.

It is a very fine watch considering the hard conditions it has to work in at present. Herbert Swift, a friend of my rival David Lewis, obtained it for me and practically gave it to me. He is a radio ham, who had one of the earliest amateur licences.

What I need now is to find a station broadcasting ice reports. I'm only 300 miles off the June 8th ice limit. I don't like ice for a yacht; it's probably because I've never had any experience of it at sea. The point is that the closer I can go to Cape Race the more favourable the Labrador current I can pick up compared with the adverse Gulf Stream–North Atlantic current farther south.

At present I'm aiming for 45° N. 50° W. as a turning point. That will shave the June 8th ice area. But if the ice patrols had found the ice area had receded I could cut a corner. On the other hand if more has come down from Greenland etc., and I don't know about it I might regret it. I don't suppose there are as many ice floes as ships anyway.

The gale has eased. It is really reprehensible meteorological tactics just when I have started serious evening drinking. I must go and re-hoist the mainsail.

I shall think before acting. We have done 53½ miles since noon and half that time under jib only so there are strong winds about.

2nd July. 1100 hrs. BST (or 7.30 St John's, Newfoundland). We are sailing again, thank God. If, last night, you guessed I was not very sound in moral fibre, you guessed right. At 0300 hrs. I decided not to hoist the mainsail although conditions were good. I released Miranda, tacked to the ssw., set the tiller as well as I could and packed up. 'She's yours for the night,' I told *Gipsy Moth.* And I think she took my word for it because several times in my half sleep I heard her turn round in a tight circle like a pup trying to catch its tail. The log only showed 9 miles during the night so I suppose she can't have gone far in the wrong direction even if she went nowhere in the right one.

I struggled out of my blankets at 0800 hrs. but I could have done with another twelve hours' sleep. I need bags of it, oceans of it and quiet restful stuff, not waking every thirty minutes to the explosion of a sea landing on the cabin top or the feel of something wrong with the sails or wind or trim.

I made some coffee before going on deck this time, but I had a bad start because I let myself be thrown across the cabin with serious detriment to my coccyx (Latin for tail), the first part of my anatomy to hit the other side of the cabin, but that is repairable whereas my Thermos is not. It not only fragmented itself but did it all over the cabin sole, where I had to spend ten minutes trying to sweep it up. At least the same cabin sole has now had a sweep-up, which I doubt if otherwise it would have got this voyage.

We are sailing very well indeed under No. 2 jib and main with the first reef rolled up. But I fear it is too good to be true. While breakfasting the wind has already veered 25° and not only are we once again headed 50° off our desired course but this veering usually seems to forerun a blow-up. Thick fog, visibility 75 yards, heavy rain showers, grey, grey, grey. Shall I ever arrive, tacking eternally like this? Oh, for a week's wind free enough to sail full and bye; it would put me right into New York, just seven days of it.

This morning I tallied up my paraffin store. I had fifty-nine bottles to start with and have used 31. How long is this trip going to be yet? I never expected to need so much in midsummer. But the Aladdin stove is on now, everything is damp in the ship if not wet. And then there is

124

Tilley, who uses a lot of paraffin (a bottle a night), but I don't want to cut her down. That glaring bright white light in the stern is a great comfort to me and most helpful if I am reefing or doing deck work. I can ease up a bit on the galley Primus and can use candles, of which I have plenty, instead of cabin lamps.

I may get put on the mat by the Board of Trade for using the Tilley but it is a practical light for a yacht. It shows up the sails well and of course a sailing vessel has right of way. over all powered vessels; it must show up miles away.

My navigation lights and masthead light are all out of action, but the red and green lights must be hard to see more than 300 yards away in a yacht at the best of times, besides which, owing to the pitching and yawing, they must be very puzzling to a steamer ahead which does spot them. Finally one of them is usually blanketed completely by a headsail when heeled.

The re-baked bread is a great success, tastes fresher and better than when new. My son, Giles, brought down eight loaves to Plymouth from London from the Mayfair bakery which I consider makes some of the best wholemeal bread I have tasted.

You may be surprised when I tell you what is the greatest success among the foods on board – I mean the solids – Bircher-Benner's Muesli.[1] Sheila brought down from London six packets already made up. It only needs some water, a grated raw apple, some lemon juice and a dessert spoon of Mr Fortnum's honey to make the most delicious breakfast. I never get tired of it. Incidentally I find I am only eating two meals a day instead of three at present.

Blast! it sounds like another squall starting.

1500 hrs. I suppose one of the greatest pleasures is simply getting over difficulties. I feel this is an incredibly naïve remark that will make you laugh comically or sardonically or in some such super-civilized manner. Go ahead then, laugh! It sifts down to just this; I feel as pleased as a

[1] The muesli which I used is called Fruti-Fort, and is made up in Switzerland. Dr Bircher-Benner's recipe was based on an ancient Swiss peasant dish, and consists of raw oats, brown sugar, wheat, barley, milk-powder, hazelnuts and sultanas.

cocker spaniel patted on the back that I lowered my main-sail in that gale-force squall, furled it so as to leave the bottom 100 square feet loose for reefing, then found it was blowing too hard to reef even the lowered sail and finally set the trysail instead. What is the point of my story? Well, frankly, I dreaded having to go out and reef that hulking great brute of a sail in another gale. Then I dreaded all the planning and messing about and hard unpleasant tricky work of setting the trysail. But it all went smoothly. Finally I came down to a cabin nicely warmed by that magician Aladdin and I found that life is extremely good. So then I said why was it good? And there we come to the conclusion I started with: the great pleasure I had got from getting over the difficulties. Yet I think they need to be the difficulties or obstacles of an adventure with a spice of danger added.

CHAPTER TEN

July 3rd to 7th

Newfoundland Time for Best Scotch – Over Flemish
Cap – Concerned with Ice – Warmer – Fishing on the
Grand Banks – The Vision of an Island – Whales –
The Tactical Dilemma of Ice – What the 'Pilot'
Says . . . – Another Gale – In a Beam Current – Cape
Race Radio Beacon – R/T Conversation in a Dream –
2,464 Miles – 500 Miles for Tacking – The Meridian
of Cape Spear – Man and his Fate – First Dinner in
America

3rd July. I took to the bottle (best Scotch) 0915 hrs. Newfoundland time, one of the earliest starts for me. I'm afraid
it weakens the story by saying this is 1245 hrs. of my time.
As soon as I fished out the bottle the weather lightened a
bit as if to admit: 'This is a fellow not to be trifled with; is
it any use our continuing with this muck of weather we
dole out on the Grand Banks if he merely starts drinking
whisky at breakfast time in retaliation?'

I had got out early this morning, lowered the trysail and
hoisted the mainsail. Besides the usual fog it was pouring
down a sub-tropical deluge. When I raised my arms above
my head to shackle on the halliard to the head of the mainsail, the water just poured up my sleeve.

I wouldn't mind so much getting wet if I could get dry
again. But almost no piece of clothing or bedding has dried
the past three weeks except for a few bits one afternoon.
Water seems to penetrate everywhere in the boat.

This morning I suddenly caught sight of a dry patch on
the cabin sole and was astonished and delighted until I
found that it was part of a potato-sack protruding from a
locker which looked like a few dry floor-boards.

All is not gloom; I had a wonderful sleep last night
thanks to the trysail. I felt it wouldn't matter if there was
another storm with that rig. It gets the ship through the

water quietly too. I was amazed on hoisting it how the slamming and banging of the bows and the slatting of the jib eased at once. She quietly presses on too.

Yesterday's run was 102½ miles and the main was up only two hours of the period. Of course there has been plenty of wind; the run the day before was 95½ miles and No. 2 jib was the only sail set for sixteen hours out of the twenty-four. I think that is surprising because we were hard on the wind all the time.

Gosh! it's cold. I must just pop out to see if there is any ice about.... Well, I wouldn't see it if there was because of the fog. What a place! Actually we are over Flemish Cap, an outlying shoal east of the Grand Banks. This morning, to continue my reasons for taking to drink, my fingers not only went all sodden white with the water but were so numb with cold that it was difficult to unscrew the shackles. And this is midsummer.

I wonder if the announcer of CBN station CBC St John's, Newfoundland, would be amused if he knew how I have been hanging on his words. He said finally: 'In twenty seconds it will be 9.15.' I rushed to my navigation watch to check it. But was the announcer looking at his watch, the station clock, or what? I feel he would not say 'twenty seconds' unless he was giving accurate time.

You must be astonished that an old hand navigator should be caught out with no means of getting a time signal. My only excuse is that the R/T set was not fitted till the afternoon before the race started and it had never occurred to me that it would not cover one of the ten or so frequencies on which wwv broadcast time signals the whole day long. I shall get by.

Having got the accurate time the next step is to use it. I fear there will be no chance of a sun sight today. The sun might show hazy in the fog overhead, but there will be no horizon to use as a datum with the fog on the sea surface. I got a snap-shot yesterday which gave me a valuable latitude and another single shot the day before which when combined with the latitude gave me something of a position indication.

But my big concern at the moment is ice. I have a chart before me as I write, on which I have plotted the ice area given for June 8th. What does 'A' do now? I am now headed for this area 60 miles away, and if we keep as we are now we shall run into it 60 miles north of its south-east corner.

I have been hoping for the south wind forecast for the Grand Banks yesterday by my announcer friend. With a south wind I could have made good a heading of south-west which would have cut across the corner of the ice area. I was delighted on waking to find the wind had gone round to the south. This was most cheering. But as soon as I went below for breakfast the wind veered again and put us back on our old heading. Maybe this ice area has shrunk since June 8th though the accumulated data shows it does not change much from June to July normally.

If only I could find out? I don't want to head off south for a day to avoid a danger which does not exist. Last night at midnight and at 0400 hrs. I tried to call up one of the ocean stations as the Atlantic weather ships now call themselves, but with no reply. What would you do in these circumstances?

I think the problem has nearly solved itself. The wind has veered further and we are now headed 330°, which is too much to the north. I wouldn't mind cutting a corner, even a big corner of this ice area but I don't think it is sensible to charge right into the middle of it. I will go and tack.

2120 hrs. BST. (1750 hrs. Newfoundland time). It is good of you to let me prattle to you. I look forward to it and also it is very dietetic; it enables me to drink plenty of fresh lemon juice which I have been many times told is so important for mariners and everyone else. Also I find it improves the whisky I take the lemon in.

Talking of whisky, whenever I'm next in a quandary, I must have whisky for breakfast. Here was I this morning full of woe and misery. As soon as the magic spirit had percolated to my farthest capillaries, what happened? I went up to tack and within an hour the fog had disappeared, the sun came out, I got some sun shots, unreefed the main and changed to the genoa, was becalmed and lowered the main because of the awful banging of sail and boom and it became hot.

I had put on a thick flannel shirt on top of my cotton one and a pair of woollen underpants and I had to strip off hurriedly, it was suddenly so intensely hot. I suppose this was an eddy of the Gulf Stream air invading the cold air of the Labrador current. Later I got the time signal from the Ottawa observatory, and more sun shots to make a sun-fix. Incidentally the St John's announcer was spot on with his times. So now all I want is a good sailing wind for ten days and no more unpleasantness.

My next objective is Sable Island, the dreaded banana-shaped island of sand which is supposed to have caused countless wrecks.[1] It seems to be uninhabited except for the lighthouse keeper. A bare low-lying sand-spit. The wrecks were partly due to the difficulty of seeing it at all but mostly because of the variable currents near by. It is in the sort of no-man's land between the Gulf Stream moving 12 to 24 miles a day eastwards and the Labrador current flowing 10 miles a day westward. The boundary varies and a ship is liable to think itself in one when it is in the other.

If I can work a passage between Sable Island and Nova Scotia I shall be sure of the Labrador current. The differ-ence whether one is in the one current or the other totals 25 miles a day on the average and that is five hours sailing a day. I've been plugging against the current all the way across the Atlantic and long to be in a favourable stream.

It is very tantalizing that this ice area prevents one from joining the west-going current sooner. However, with luck, in three days I shall get into a negative beam-on current followed soon after by a favourable one. But this Labrador stream does entail fog. It has already returned here. And it may persist for another 800 miles. It does seem a long way, the log reads 2,054 miles tonight and still there is at a rough guess 1,300 miles to do. And at the moment we are nearly becalmed. I must look out my fishing-tackle. If this is the world's most famous fishing-ground, fresh fish for breakfast is a possibility.

4th July. 0930 hrs. St John's Newfoundland time. I have changed my clocks at last; it became too bizarre having daylight past midnight and waking up in the dark at

[1] See map of Sable Island wrecks, p. 35.

0800 hrs. Speaking of time, I was trying in the middle of the night to call an ocean weather station ship and while passing the switch through the channel labelled Boston, I suddenly got a wwv signal loud and clear from the Bureau of Standards sending out their twenty-four-hours-a-day time signal. I tried again this morning but not a sound. I suppose it was reflected off the heaviside layer during the night.

My R/T set gives a very good reception when it does pick up a station. It is a question of range. Look how St John's came in loud and clear though only the day before there was not a sound. At night the range is considered to be doubled. I wish I could get an ice report; that is really all I want from the radio at the moment. I can't see any point in trying to report my position now. No, I'm wrong there, Sheila and my friends may be anxious about my silence. I will keep on trying to get a message through.

If you come around to the Grand Banks in a year's time you may see me there still tacking against light head-winds and against the current. My position has not changed much in two days. At present I'm doing 1⅛ knots in a direction I don't want to go, with a current of ½ knot against me from the direction in which I do want to go. St John's radio forecasts a southerly wind on the Grand Banks today which would suit me fine, but they say it will become a sw. this afternoon, which is again right in the eye from New York.

The only thing to do is to relax and enjoy oneself if one can. I have found the remains of a bottle of sherry and a jar of pickled gherkins, but I don't think sherry is a sea drink. This afternoon I must do some housework or go fishing or both.

2030 hrs. St John's time. I had two surprises today. The first was when I saw a long low island in the foggy mist. As a navigator thinking himself 360 miles from the nearest land, you can imagine I was surprised. Visibility had improved and was about a mile. It was in fact a big swell looming in the mist. One doesn't notice the movements of these big swells at all in a small boat and I had not seen them before because of the thick fog.

The fog cleared today and it was clear and sunny, but we were at once becalmed. I am not happy tonight. I

131

measured the distance still to go as 1,340 miles and we have sailed 18 miles in the past fourteen hours, and not even in the right direction. I spent part of the day doing my housework, checking over the stores, throwing out mouldy oranges, etc. I find I have only three bottles of meths left. Tilley light has been an unexpected drain on meths. I have plenty of water; my big tank of 35 gallons is nearly full and I did not bother to measure the other one which I am still using.

I had some difficulty in lifting the wooden trap in the cabin sole to inspect the water tank. The floor boards are jammed tight together with the wet. Underneath, the boards were mildewed. But that's nothing; when I came to sweep out the cabin I found mildew all over the place on the cabin sole, under the table etc. What can one expect with no drying air for three weeks, and wet pouring in through every opening and cranny.

I fished. I could not leave the Grand Banks (but shall I ever leave them?) without fishing first. I used a feather lure with no success and then I tried a mackerel spinner with no more success. That reminds me of my second surprise. I heard a sort of deep sigh and came up on deck for a look-see during dinner.

Fifteen feet away four whales dived beneath the surface. I could have prodded one with a boathook. They looked awfully black and sleek and powerful and my first thought was 'Are you friendly?' I was puzzled when I had had a good look. They were smaller than the 70 feet one expects a whale to be but much too big for the kind of porpoise I have met. I think they were 15 to 25 feet long. They were very black looking; would they be blackfish? I suppose they are all whales but one thinks of a 70-foot sperm or suchlike when whale is mentioned. I estimated there were about a hundred of them.

I pulled in my log as fast as I could in case of accident to it. Besides, it would be bad for the whale's digestion. I concluded too that this was a broad hint that the fishing-ground here was exclusively theirs. I took the hint and hauled in my tackle. My impression was that all or most of all the whales in the pack came up in turn to investigate *Gipsy Moth* and then after ten minutes or a quarter of an hour as if at a signal, they all dived together and vanished. I have seldom known a yachtsman to fish. Especially an ocean racer. I wonder why. I think perhaps that the life on the sea makes one friendly towards everything living in it. I know this afternoon I was secretly hoping I wouldn't catch anything, although the old hunting-instinct made me keen to try. Civilization has knotted us up in this respect. What about fishermen though? I can't work it out.

I set my ghoster genoa when there was a zephyr at the end of the calm. I have never used it before. It set beautifully and pulled quite hard when there was not enough wind to make Miranda move at all. That reminds me I must go and change it to the heavy genoa before it is quite dark. I don't want to risk it being pulled out of shape by a strong wind while I am asleep.

2200 hrs. It is lovely at present, calm sea, fine cloud formation and a gibbous moon showing through, twilight just turning to dark, the ship gliding through the water with a silky rustle, a squeaky bird flying about and making queer squeaky mewing sounds when I show a light as if it wanted to talk.

We are headed about ssw. but I am hoping the wind will veer shortly and put the ship on to a westerly course without waking me up. I think we have gone far enough south now to avoid the ice. I assume it must have receded somewhat northwards since the June 8th report.

5th July. 0925 hrs. St John's time. That was a good sail last night. 58½ miles in 9 hours, of which 5 hours at 7 knots. You may well say, 'Why don't I always sleep if Miranda and *Gipsy Moth* get on so well when I'm not there?' I must tell you that the period was not without its pangs for me. First I woke at midnight and found we had crept round to a southerly heading, so retrimmed sails and Miranda's lines. It was dense fog so I lit Tilley and rigged her with Old Faithful, the riding light still alight in the stern.

At 0043 hrs. I was out again and noted how hard it was to trim for a beam wind. I hovered till 0130 and then tried for some more sleep. I was expecting the wind to shift during the night from se. to south and later to shift again from south to south-west according to the St John's broadcast forecast. I hoped the ship would peacefully follow these changes round and that I should wake in the morning to find the heading north-west. Super optimist!

At 0215 I woke feeling drugged with sleep but answering to an uneasy feeling. It was pouring a tropical downfall of heavy rain. During this cascade the wind lulled preparatory to a shift in direction. Unfortunately, I had left a shock-cord with tension on the tiller to bias it to weather, and thereby help Miranda. As soon as the wind dropped, Miranda ceased to pull the tiller but the shock-cord still did and we began to gybe. I was most anxious to avoid this to save Miranda from getting tangled up with the backstay and main boom.

I jumped out of bed and slipped an oilskin coat over me but had no time for the trousers, boots or cap. So there I was bare-footed, bare-headed, and in my long woollen underfugs, God bless 'em . . . in a cockpit which already was 3 inches deep in water and bucketfuls emptying on top of me. What a jolly life the mariner has!

I saved the possible lash-up and got everything going well and I must say my blankets did seem even more cosy than before when I returned with numb feet, etc., etc. This was at 0215 and after that I was allowed to sleep in peace till 0725 while Miranda and *Gipsy Moth* knocked up 7 knots average. I find I have learnt a lot about sailing this voyage, especially in regard to sail-trimming; I find it fascinating, though often I wish I did not have to learn it the hard way as last night.

With the shortage of fuel and abundance of wet clothes I have picked up one or two miserly tricks to help me counteract the shortage. Whenever the Primus flame is unoccupied I put on a big pot of salt water. This is expected to radiate heat after the fire is out and is very helpful with drying dish-cloths which I spread over the hot saucepan.

Now I'm trying a development of this; I filled Sheila's hot-water bottle and wrapped a wet pair of trousers round it. If this is a success I could repeat it every time I light the Primus and gradually dry out a few bits of clothing. I also found that a hot kettle on the cabin sole dried out a patch underneath it and as it can stand just as well down there as on the stove I plan to move it about a small area beside my berth in the hope I can have a wee area of dry boards to step on.

Now I am in a tactical dilemma. It all hinges again on this ice question. It really is tantalizing to think of the special USA ice patrol vessels out all the time to locate bergs and mark the limits of small ice. No one could wish for their information more than I do and I cannot get the merest whisper about it. I regularly comb the whole range of frequencies available to me but no joy.

The tactical problem is this (wait till I get the chart): On my present heading I shall be into the June 8th ice area in nine hours' time. If I tack then it will put me on the less favourable heading. On this present tack we are headed 30° to the right of New York. But if I tack on reaching the ice area we shall be headed 70° to the left of New York.

Furthermore, if I could continue into the aforesaid ice area for 120 miles after entering it, I would get into the favourable Labrador current which will help me on my way round Cape Race. I think I should be lucky not to run into ice during that further 120 miles.

Let us see what the Admiralty Pilot says about it. This is the Novia Scotia volume which covers the Grand Banks; it has 14 pages dealing with ice only. 'The worst season for bergs in the Great Bank region is from the middle of March to the middle of July.' 'The greater number take the deep water route, Path C, down the eastern edge of the Bank and these constitute the greatest danger to the shipping routes.'

At the moment I am bang in the middle of route C, crossing it. (Just wait while I have a look-out for icebergs from the cockpit, will you!) Reading this stuff I half expected to see a berg but as the visibility is only 200 yards in the fog at present I rustled back to my cosy seat below.

Then the 'Pilot' says 'The normal number of bergs south of the 48th parallel of latitude' (we are at 45° 40′ at the moment) is June, 14; July, 25, and south of the 43rd parallel June, 12; July, 3.' Therefore I consider I can expect the June 8th area to have shrunk a great deal by July 5th (because there are only one-third as many bergs in the area in July compared with June).

I hope you don't mind me reasoning this out on paper with you; it seems to clarify the issue. The Pilot gives a plan for each month of the year, and these show that the 'probable mean limit of bergs and growlers, 1920–1939' recedes about 150 miles northwards in July compared with June; also that I shall be through the southern tongue of this area by the 47° 30′ w. meridian which I am due to reach at 1730 hrs. this evening.

On the whole the paper evidence is strongly in favour of its being all right. The only doubt left in my mind is raised by the cold. I have my woollies on, the Aladdin stove going at its highest flame, the ventilator bunged up and the doors shut, yet it is cold below. Above on deck, it is freezing cold with thick fog, visibility 100 yards.

Well, thank you. I've made up my mind that it *is* reasonable to press on. I shall put my trust in the Almighty who I am convinced has it all arranged anyhow. I will now fetch out the Guinness.

It is fine to be sailing again and approximately in the right direction. If only I could have twelve days of this wind it would put me in New York. I wonder where my rivals are? I sometimes think these races would be much improved in excitement and interest by knowing where all the rivals are. This is done in the Sydney–Hobart race where positions are all recorded daily.

But there is another way of looking at it from the competitor's viewpoint. If he knew his rival was hopelessly far ahead, it might spoil his fun that he gets hoping to the end that he may be first even if actually last; while on the other hand, if he hears his rivals have all packed up through accidents or got hopelessly far behind, that could spoil his sport even more.

One of the things I have learnt on this race is that a yacht with a self-steering device could never compete with a fully crewed one. I never realized how frequently one changed the trim of the sails or the sails themselves in racing; or put another way, how the wind direction and speed are changing nearly the whole time.

This Atlantic race is much dependent on the endurance of the man. Had I twice my endurance, twice my strength and twice my 'what-it-takes' I would have many times changed sails when I didn't and carried more canvas than I did, and many, many times more often I would have retrimmed.

It will be fascinating to me to see how my black-bearded friend has got along. I can't see him turning over in his berth determined to get some more sleep while the ship heads in the wrong direction. Anyway this mucking about off the Grand Banks the past few days has given me the rest I badly needed and all I want now, I feel, is wind . . . wind . . . wind, and it can be – Hey! Press on! for New York!

6th July. 0930 hrs. What a fantastic change of life, not only physical but mental and moral too! This time last night I was fast asleep snug among the blankets. A feeling of urgency, of apprehension woke me.

Ten minutes later I was standing in two inches of water in the cockpit (in rubber boots); I got up to the mast, clipped my belt to a halliard and wrestled with the mainsail halliard in one hand to slack it away as required, grabbing handfuls of mainsail with the other hand to pull the main down as I let the halliard go up. The wind, blowing gale force, bound the sail and its slides against anything they touched so that it was hard pulling to get it down.

The bows lifted in the air and smacked down 10 feet to dash a hose of water over my back. Flashes of lightning made the fog brightly luminous. There was no sound of thunder above the sail's own thunderclaps as it flogged in the wind. The rain was a deluge but I didn't notice that or didn't distinguish it from the seawater hitting me.

The ship lurched, pitched, rolled, trying every trick to throw me from my hold. Standing on top of the dinghy to gather the sail to the boom, the seething white water from the ship's bow-waves rushed past at what seemed a terrific speed in the dark. One moment I was looking down at it from a height and the next it was quite close to me again near my own level.

Between flashes of lightning, the Tilley light threw my giant shadow on to the fog behind me. It was exhilarating, hanging on, doing the job, while tearing through the darkness rushing into nothing ahead. But the sudden change

137

from being warm and drowsy with sleep makes it a hard life. The first time I went up was to change to a smaller jib, next I went up to change the main for a trysail but when the main was furled we were going so fast that I did not set the trysail.

To show there was some wind, at my third sortie from the blankets which was in daylight, we had travelled 25 miles at a speed of 6·1 knots under No. 2 jib only. This time I set the trysail and it is still set but I must go and change back to the mainsail as the wind has abated.

I remember how apprehensive I felt before turning in last night. At that time we were having a wonderful sail, going fast over a calm sea. I was not happy last night about charging blindly into the night, in dense fog, visibility 75 yards. I've always understood the Grand Banks are the greatest fishing-grounds of the world and must be stuffed with trawlers. Far more trawlers than even icebergs I would think. Instinct is a creepy, scared, shrinking little funk. I told it as firmly as I could that the Grand Banks are a huge area more than 200 miles square, and that if you shoot into a covey of partridges you never bag one. Therefore why worry about a trawler on the Grand Banks?

All the same I shall be thankful to be off them. What a place! Well! up and doing! I must not waste any of this wind.

I went up and decided to reef before hoisting the main. I hate that reefing; it is hard work, tedious and needs much attention. I would say 1½ hours of hard grind on one's own to do it thoroughly, an hour anyhow.

By that time the wind had strengthened and I decided there was plenty of it for the trysail. There might not be too much for the fully reefed mainsail as it is but if it increases a little more (as in fact I hear now by the rising whine, that it has) then I have all the work to undo and the trysail to reset.

So here I am back in the snuggery. I will send for the steward to bring me my morning Guinness. But seriously, on looking into it further, I find that we are doing 5⅓ knots hard on the wind with the trysail set and I relax when that is set. Half this race is a matter of keeping out of trouble and unnecessary work. We have sailed 134½ miles this day so far with half an hour to go to noon. Not bad, with four hours of it under jib only and four under jib and trysail. Oh! for a week of it, which would see me into New York!

I must get weaving on the navigation. This charging through fog for days on end with no chance of a fix needs careful dead reckoning. I did not make navigating easier yesterday by dropping and breaking my navigation watch. Now I must use the electric clock.

I noted down every time mentioned by the CBC announcer, called Jeff Scott, before breakfast. I got nine times from him which made my clock between five and twenty seconds fast. The average was twelve seconds fast and if I use that I shall be probably not more than two miles out. As there does not seem the least possibility of a sun sight because of the fog it does not matter much at present.

PS. A horrid whine in the rigging; what luck that I was confiding in you and didn't go up half an hour earlier to set the main. I should have been taking it down again only a few minutes after finishing the job. Do you recommend some oranges or Guinness for my elevenses?

Later. Yesterday's run 137 miles, total miles to date 2,355. Big news for me, we are in a beam current, i.e. no longer bucking a head-on current, and tomorrow we should enter the south-west going Labrador current which I hope we shall carry all the way to New York. We are 140 miles ESE. of Cape Race and I hope by tomorrow will have a bit of the American continent behind us.

7th July. 1125 hrs. St John's time. I've gone and taken a lot of the pleasure out of my morning prattle to you by washing up the breakfast things (and dinner and supper and 2nd, 3rd and 4th suppers included of course). I only realized when I had done it how much more I enjoyed my prattle if I was feeling I ought to have washed up but hadn't.

I nearly lost my head this morning and rushed down to write that it was a fine day, sun shining, water sparkling, clear cut horizon all round. I began pondering which department of stores and gear I would bundle out first for

139

drying. Luckily my natural caution restrained me – we are in fog again.

I'm sure we will have a fine day before reaching New York, though it just doesn't seem credible at the moment. Last night Chichester the Great Marine Technician came unstuck again. No, sorry, it was this morning, though it seems like yesterday. I got up at 4 a.m. to do the rounds and see that all my crew were awake and doing their British duty while the captain slept.

We had reached the most unfavourable heading on the port (north-west) tack. Any more veer of the wind made the other tack (south-west heading) more favourable.

I had a tin of Heinz's tomato soup to make the brain souple (pardon!) and worked out some brilliant tactics on the following premises: If the wind veered any more this tack would not only be bad but it would use up valuable northing. By my estimate and experience the principal wind is west-south-west from a few degrees south of where I want to go, therefore the port (north-west) tack tends to be more favourable than the other. Therefore I am more often on it and therefore always tend to angle off to the north. If last night I went off on the northerly tack without need it would be wasting valuable northing.

The Met. forecaster yesterday in St John's said the wind would veer to the north-west. Although I nearly always regret acting on a Met. forecast, this one sounded infallible. So I put on my armour and tacked. The idea was that while I slept the ship now headed 235° (about sw. by w.) would gently come round, while I slept, to 290°, the heading I wanted.

Alas! when I awoke at nine o'clock, the sun streaming in through the cabin ports, the ship was headed 210°, which is really due south true direction because the magnetic variation is 27° (the wind instead of shifting on to north-west had moved back towards south-west).

This is saddening to the heart of a racing man. The only consolation I could find for myself was that I couldn't keep on the north-westerly tack for ever however much more favourable it might be. I mean, one can't just charge through Newfoundland, can one? even if it is on the favourable tack.

140

Last night my mind was twisting about mostly asleep. I would try to contact Cape Race on the R/T. I would tell him I got a bearing of his radio beacon (which I did) yesterday, with my Heron-Homer set and how delighted I was to find the beacon working. I had been told the American (USA and Canadian) beacons were no use, too feeble and ineffective. It was a great moment when I picked up Cape Race Beacon loud and clear after a 1,500-mile beacon silence.

Now I need not worry about my loss of accurate time-keeping because a bearing from Cape Race would replace the longitude sextant shot and I could always get a latitude to cross the Cape Race position line for a fix. The latitude sight is independent of accurate time because at noon the sun is at the top of its path across the sky and does not change altitude appreciably for a few minutes.

In my dream the Cape Race man kept on saying angrily . . . 'But we have three beacons with a 100-inch range not just one.' Then I was running over (asleep, still, I suppose) what I should say in a message to Chris Brasher of the *Observer* . . . give some of the reasons for being so damn long: such as . . . 'Had to tack nearly whole way across the Atlantic against headwinds . . .' or 'Delayed by headwinds, storm and repairs.' Or would the facetious touch be better? 'Arrived Cape Race. Lovely sail. Still weigh 154 pounds and doing well. Advise my wife will be late for dinner.'

Calms can be much harder work than a blow, I think. Last evening I was involved in a grand calm shemozzle. Bang over comes the boom as the ship rolls. Down mainsail.

I had made the awful mistake of not securing the main boom before lowering the sail. As I had rushed up from below I had caught sight of part of Miranda damaged; it was an outhaul for the spanker which had parted right out at the end of the spanker boom which is out of reach. This distracted my attention and I let the mainsail down with a run. Over came the boom, whang! against the weather-side runner. Bang! back again. Whang! into the runner again. My heart was in my throat; that boom must weigh a good hundredweight and is about 18 feet long and the whole ship shuddered as it hit the runner each time.

I came scrambling back making a firm resolution (which I shall never keep) that I would never lower the main without first securing the boom. However, Fate may have been on my side after all. Miranda's outhaul had bust before the calm and if there had been any wind at all I would have had to dismantle the spanker and spanker boom to reach and repair the end.

Now with the calm I was able to swivel the whole mast and sail round and secure it to the main boom and backstay while I made the necessary repairs. I worked in a bit of a flap to get the job done urgently.

A very gentle breeze got up before I finished and even with that the strain on Miranda held against the breeze to the mainboom was considerable. Her sail area is 45 square feet. With the mildest of winds I would have had to release her and unrig all the spanker gear to make the repair. As it was I just succeeded in completing the job as the breeze arrived. Then up with the main again, change the jib for the genoa and off we go.

In spite of the calm we sailed 109½ miles yesterday and the total sailed to date is 2,464 miles plus about 50 unlogged. I make it 2,000 miles by direct great circle route from Plymouth Hoe to Cape Race, so the tacking against headwinds has cost me 500 extra miles sailing. And of course the ship's speed is much slower when on the wind than when reaching or running.

1935 hrs. In fifteen minutes I am due to cross the meridian of the easternmost point of North America, namely Cape Spear.

(Extract from log: At 2005 July 7 I crossed the meridian of Cape Spear the eastern-most point of North America 26 days 12 hours 35 minutes of actual time after leaving Plymouth Hoe. Distance 2,000 miles to a mile. Average distance made good, 75 miles per day. Average distance sailed, 94 miles per day.)

I feel this calls for a big celebration; I shall have to open a tin of sardines or indulge in some similar orgy. I shall try once more to call up a shore station or ship to send news of my position. I had no luck last night. I'm beginning to wonder if the GPO took out the crystal of the 2182 channel as well as those of the other channels. This they did because it was an American set which had not been licensed for use in British waters.

I would have expected Cape Race to hear me last night. They are only 55 miles away and all ships and stations are supposed to guard this frequency for three minutes at the hour and half hour for any S O S calls. . . .

Maybe my Fate does not wish me to get this message through. There was a bang on the deck behind where I am sitting in the cabin. I darted up to see what had bust and it was the big glass insulator of the R/T aerial. The wire had bust and the insulator hit the deck with no uncertain bang. It weighs about a pound.

Later I wasn't quite sure about Fate and the R/T. I've never been able to make up my mind what is the relationship between man and his Fate; so I put on my long boots and oilskin coat and went and mended the aerial. I'll let you know later what happens. If it is working someone must hear me when only 50 miles offshore.

It has been a lovely day for me. Not a single alarum or excursion all day. The fog cleared off as silently as it stole in, the sun shone and the horizon stayed sharp and clear. We have quietly reeled off 40 miles since noon though the ship does not seem to be moving. It is extraordinary how at 5⅓ knots which we have averaged we might have been ghosting along at 1 knot it was so quiet, while if the speed goes up 1⅛ knots to 6½ knots the racket is infernal . . . bashing, crashing, banging, lurching, pitching and rolling. I could do with two days of this; a lovely sleep after each meal, peace, quiet. I reckon I need it.

I tried for a good half hour this morning to fish out a knurled nut lodged in the non-return valve of the cockpit drain. I wanted to get it out before tacking when the water would flood in. It was an awful fiddly job fishing for it out of sight with a bit of bent wire in each hand. In the end I gave up.

I'm only telling the story of the knurled nut to illustrate how it pays to give up provided you don't do so for too long. Later, I got an idea, lashed a matchstick to each jaw of a clothes peg and recovered the nut easily. If you knew what I've suffered waddling in a flooded cockpit due to that nut you would forgive my smug story.

143

Bad news on the domestic front. I got round to inspecting the coats etc. hanging in the compartment made for them. My two reefer jackets, my velvet smoking and black trousers were soaking wet and covered in mildew. By some miracle Sheila's things hanging with them including her white and blue striped trousers seem quite all right. I put her oilskin coat over the top of her knitted coat and trousers. Seems an obvious thing to do, doesn't it, when there is wet about.

Now to serious business, my first dinner in America.

13a   Hanking on No. 2 after lowering the ghoster near Ambrose Light

13b   The storm caught me with these twin spinnakers set

14   A wave from Sheila: I still don't know if I've won or lost

CHAPTER ELEVEN

July 8th to 13th

Heavenly Morning – Talking to Cape Race – End of
Four Weeks' Silence – Orgy of Cleanliness – Whale
Deep (Kipling) – Favourable Current – Message from
Chris – News of Rivals – Halcyon Conditions – Met.
Forecasts Should be Abolished! – Sable Island Beacon
– On a Broad Reach – Apprehension – Charging at the
Coast in Fog – Blunder with the Charts – Discrepancy
of DR and Observation – Warm and Muggy – More
Whales – Calling Up Halifax – The Suspicious Opera-
tor – Ticked Off by Primus

8th July. 0600 hrs. St John's time. I can hardly believe it.
I found myself looking around for something to do next.
It is a lovely, a heavenly morning. Calm clear sky. Sun up
bright and early. We have been ghosting along all night
and sailed 25½ miles between my visits to the cockpit. It's
true we are only ambling along at 3¾ knots but up to date
I could not enjoy anything more.

A glorious sleep from 2300 hrs. till 0500 hrs. when I
rolled a drowsy eye round to the tell-tale compass, noted
we were headed north and very reluctantly dressed to tack
ship. However, by the time I had dressed and coffeed, the
tell-tale had reverted to 340° which is still a paying course.
I think it was a little trick to get me out of my berth, because now it is back to 305°, which is only 9° off the heading we want.

I tried calling up a shore station but with no luck. Instead, I picked up wwv loud and clear on the Boston
channel and got a good check of my electric clock. It is a
wonderful timekeeper considering for one thing it has a
second-hand about 4 inches long. My only criticism is that
the minute-hand must be a little loose and that it flops

over half a minute as it turns through top centre, 60th minute.

0830 hrs. Excitement! I contacted Cape Race on the R/T. The operator was very patient and took down a message to the *Observer* in which I asked them to advise Sheila in New York. It is quite an odd feeling of excitement to speak to someone after four weeks' silence. I said I would call back at 2100 hrs. tonight.

1530 hrs. I lost my head this morning with all the excitement and fun, and I went in for an absolute orgy of cleanliness. I not only shaved – and really a self-binding harvester would have been more suitable than my Gillette razor – but I had a terrific bath. This is my name for a wash in toto.

I followed the detergent directive and first worked up a good lather followed by three thorough rinsings. I don't know whether this operation was a shock to the system, but I was extremely cold all the morning afterwards. I navigated sitting on my berth, not only wearing cotton underpants, woollen fug-pants and flannel trousers but covered up with two blankets as well. Labrador current! this ought to be called the Arctic current. I think the fog which soon turned up after breakfast was the real culprit; through the 'precipitation' as the Met. emperors like to call it, everything gets damp. I could see a small stream of water leaving the main boom at the clew of the sail.

At lunch time I had to tack to the ssw.; reluctantly because the wnw. tack was still the better but for one thing I was headed straight for an area I happened to hear broadcast by St John's radio yesterday as being scheduled for us Air Force bombing and rocket firing practice during July. It was only 10 miles away when I tacked. I have been shot at, or over, a number of times by British and French guns while in a yacht and dislike it. Though really the nearest to a hit was a shell which landed 50 yards away. I often wonder why but will never know I suppose. I don't wish to try out an American gunner's aim!

The second reason for tacking was that this leg was pushing me up into Cabot Strait and if (the third reason) the wind shifts to the sw., as forecast this morning, while I am up in Cabot Strait, I could not continue on a westerly

146

tack but would have to head south or worse, which would be a pity.

We passed 9 miles to one side of the Whale Deep on the Grand Banks. Rudyard Kipling in his book *Captains Courageous* about the fishing-life on the Grand Banks mentions the Whale Deep and has a laugh at one of the characters who tries to anchor in it.

I got great satisfaction that at last I am in a favourable current which is quietly working away on my behalf (I hope) wafting me south-westwards. It is however said to be very capricious.

I got a fix by two radio beacon bearings and a sun-shot after the fog cleared and that indicates a drift of 18 miles north-west instead of south-west yesterday. If I keep a note of these discrepancies day by day and later average them out I should get an approximate value for the set of this current. But dead reckoning with Miranda at the helm may or may not be accurate enough for such results. Obviously she cannot let me know when she changes course while I am asleep but on the other hand I suspect that, once she is properly trimmed and set up she keeps that particular heading relative to the wind direction more accurately than, say, I would if I were at the helm.

2150 hrs. I got a message from Chris Brasher through Cape Race. The gist of it was that Hasler had been sighted to the north. I knew he was set on going far north. Howells and Lacombe went via the Azores. That leaves Lewis, and I did not get the reference to him. There was something about 47. Does that mean he is at the 47th meridian, because if so he is only 300 miles behind me? I shall have to try and shake him off. I can almost smell the sweet blossom of antiseptic. You never know with a race till the end.

That black-bearded pirate could easily steal up from the 46th parallel if he has avoided all our bad weather up north, which he might well have done. Nor would he get so many headwinds. It is 600 miles farther by the Azores but I have done already 600 more miles in extra tacking due to headwinds.

I can easily strike days of calm off the USA coast in July; it is normal. I hope by keeping some distance offshore that
147

I can avoid some of them. According to the St John's forecast, tomorrow will not be one of those calm days anyhow because a Force 6 wind (30 m.p.h.) is due here. I am keeping on the sw. tack all night so that if this wind does blow from the sw. as forecast, I can head west and it will suit me.

It seems incredible tonight that a Force 6 is due in a few hours. In a cloudless sky the sun went down over a bright clear horizon and there is a full moon peeking in at me through the cabin port. I have not got very far today but it has been a great day to laze and get plenty of sleep. There won't be much relaxation if there are gales on the way down the coast because of the nearness to land.

I think we must have entered an eddy of the Gulf Stream about midday because it suddenly warmed up and I began stripping off some of my winter wear. The sea looked blue instead of grey and its temperature was 54° F. I think it was more like 40° this morning and regret I did not measure it.

By the way, Chris said the *Mauretania* had 'heard' me. He wanted more information about my happenings and ETA (expected time of arrival) at New York. This I am very loath to give; I hated giving ETA's when flying. As the Cape Race man could not hear me I am relieved for the moment. On this tack the aerial touches the sail and I expect that is why he could not hear me. Yet I can receive well enough.

9th July. 1100 hrs. To be candid this is the moment when I had secretly hoped I should be sailing (lee rail under, of course) past the Ambrose Light vessel at the finish of the race 28 days after the start and I find I have 900 miles still to go. I wouldn't be sorry if it were 9,900 if the sailing were all like this, the scene was so ideal a short while ago, sparkling blue sea, sun shining bright in a cloudless sky, clear-cut horizon, calm sea. I felt the word 'halcyon' should be applied but unfortunately I can't remember what it means. What a superb night too!

2225 hrs. was my last log entry last night. Rigged Old Faithful (the wonder riding light). Sailing well. Suppose I shall be called up in the night. It was past eight o'clock next morning – 9½ hours later before I resurfaced – and

148

even after that long sleep I moaned and groused that I could not sleep on another six hours.

I had rolled a bleary eye round to the tell-tale compass, and found it reading, horrors! 160°, i.e. east of south on the compass and actually south-east true direction – practically on my way home again! Though, thank heaven the heading had not been that for long because Bleary-Eye had informed me at five o'clock that it was still the same as when I turned in. That's one good thing the Met. forecaster has done for me. I certainly would not have kept on the southerly leg all night if it had not been to gain something in anticipation of the sou-westerly blow he predicted. And therefore I would not have had my gorgeous nap.

The Met. chaps work one up into a regular tiz. This morning, for example, I had some clothes out to dry and was eating my breakfast in the sun in the cockpit when a line of cloud advanced on us and the wind increased a little from Force 2, just a whiff or two more. Because of the Met. forecast I at once bundled all the clothes below followed by myself, closed down the forehatch and began debating whether I could finish my coffee before donning oilskins. So far, an hour later, nothing has happened. If it hadn't been for the forecast I would not have taken the least notice of the wee puff. So doth the Met. forecast make cowards of us all.

I'm afraid this has aroused one of the bees in my bonnet. I once gave a talk at the Institute of Navigation that Met. forecasting should be abolished for the good of aviation. Briefly the theme was: (1) only a proportion of forecasts are correct. It may be a big proportion like 75% but the point is it is not 100%. (2) If the bad forecast is wrong you have perhaps missed an opportunity to do something . . . fly, sail, or what-you-will which otherwise you would have done carefree. (3) If a good forecast goes wrong you may be very much worse off, dangerously so, than without one because you go unprepared for bad weather.

However, I had better not be smug too soon. It is only 1140 and though Force 2 still prevails, a sudden change to Force 6 would still hand the laugh to the Met. Service this time.

Chris Brasher last night asked me one or two questions

I was not keen to answer. I had plenty of time to think about a reply because I think the aerial touches the sail when on the starboard tack and the transmission is too bad to hear then. But when I tacked this morning I thought up a reply and tried to call up Cape Race.

I need not have worried because I could get no reply at all. The set is only supposed to have a range of 50 miles by day and this was 110 miles away.

I was sorry in a way because I had at last concocted a reply which I approved. Here it is: (He asked details of the damage to *Gipsy Moth* in the storm and my ETA, New York.) 'Thanks. Breakage of stanchion fastenings was unimportant but damage to steering vane was serious and inaccessible except to monkey. Took on role of monkey for several hours. Result success and thirsty monkey. For ETA supply accurate weather forecast, but try nineteenth.'

I mentioned Old Faithful just now. I must tell you a little about him. Have you ever had trouble with riding lights, by the way? Previously I had a most complicated one which took a long time to take apart in order to light and after all the tedious operation a good snatch at the anchor chain and a snubbing of the stem put the damn thing out in a twink.

Old Faithful, which John Tyrrell supplied with the boat is the most simple-looking lantern and I laughed when I first lit it. The little flame whickered away inside its glass cage, the most delicate little weakling and in fact if I took it out to adjust the wick anything but the slowest movement of the hand put it out immediately. Yet it whickered its way through that storm with no trouble at all. It only needs about an eggcupful of paraffin a night compared with the whole bottle which Tilley demands.

Well, I must set about my chores. Noon; day's run 114. This is not bad really considering we were only ambling the whole time. Is it the tortoise-hare affair or due to the owner being asleep for half the period? We have only done more than 114 in the day's run on seven days this voyage. It is extraordinary to me because this boat should easily average 5½ knots, which amounts to 132 miles. A calm of two hours, a very modest ration per day, would necessitate that the average speed for the remaining twenty-two hours should increase to 6 knots. This takes some doing in a small boat, especially if there is any sea running. Why we ambled so well yesterday is due to the calm sea, I expect. Total logged 2,677.

1930 hrs. Don't laugh! the Met. man nearly had me on toast. The wind got up to Force 5 about 1400 hrs. I changed down the genoa and it was fascinating how the ship ceased to bury her bows in the seas with the lesser foresail. Also the thumping and slamming eased, the mainsail was drawing much better whereas before it was nearly empty like a flag about to wave. Lastly, the speed went up from 4·9 knots to 6⅓ knots with the smaller sail area.

The wind was increasing and I felt sure I should be called out again as soon as I started lunch and I made a resolution to have no reefing nonsense but to switch straight away to the trysail. However it has calmed down again. Do you think the Met. man carried the day? He influenced all my actions from the time of his broadcast yesterday. His wind was not so serious. Force 5 instead of 6 and arriving p.m. instead of a.m.

The sea looks glacier blue and I felt sure it must be ice-bred water, but the temperature is 56°, which I would have thought too high. I must look up in the Pilot to see what it says about it.

I picked up Sable Island beacon this afternoon 200 miles ahead. Sable Island has always been rather a thrilling, ominous island for me.

I cannot find anything conclusive about the Labrador current temperature. The Pilot remarks the extraordinary change of temperature when the Labrador meets the Gulf Stream and says 'a change from 54° to 32° F. has been recorded in less than a ship's length.' Ah, here is something – 'On the Arctic side of the Cold Wall the colour is olive or bottle green, on the Gulf Stream side it is indigo blue.' I think my glacier water blue cannot be Gulf Stream indigo.

I am trying to pick up fresh broadcasting stations to give me the weather ahead. I consider my moral fibre has had a bad bruising from what I have had to listen to on various local broadcasting stations. Having no programme I have had to bear many hours of 1950 vintage crooning and 1940 jazz, not to mention the advertisements, in order to wait for a weather forecast and time signal. How the announcers who seem to have attractive personalities stand up to it all day is interesting. I suppose they become impervious to it.

I hope I shall pick up Halifax tomorrow as I think they make a feature of weather information. Please don't get me wrong; I like to know what the *actual* weather is all round.

2215 hrs. The wind has freed us! Backed to the south and put us on a broad reach. It is most exhilarating after being on the wind. Bash! Bash! Bash! Always pinching to head as near the objective as possible – tedious, hard, noisy sailing right across the Atlantic. The sea is moderate enough and *Gipsy Moth* is fairly scuttling along. 'I'm in a hurry' she is saying, 'let me go!' The gear at the end of the main boom makes a snaffley, clinky sound like the bridle and bit of a horse.

Standing on the stern, rigging Old Faithful the riding light, it was like standing at the end of a train, the glacier blue flood seemed to be swirling past so fast. We have done 24½ miles the past 3½ hours at 7 knots or 8 m.p.h. It is lovely sailing. As I ate my four kippers and four potatoes with four glasses of whisky I thought how lucky I was and wished 4,000 people could be enjoying a supper as much.

10th July. 1045 hrs. Really, I could easily believe that someone stood behind me and watched what I was writing so as to have a big laugh at me. I had scarcely finished my last sentence last night when I went on deck and after a good look round did something I very rarely do – put on all my oilskins, boots, sou-wester – all the works, and waited.

Horrible-looking dense black things hung in the sky in several places. They were like palls of dense black oily smoke which have risen widely apart and spread leisurely in the sky. I thought they were violent squalls and was surprised when we shot under the first one, going now at express speed, without anything happening.

Dazzling white sheet lightning appeared ahead and away to the north. We were going as fast as we could and I sat in the cockpit not wanting to cut short this lovely sail.

However, with a full load of wind already in the sails a sudden additional squall might mean breakages. I loosed off a post-prandial sigh and went forward to the mast to down the main.

One takes a much rosier view from the security and part shelter of the cockpit. At the mast I had to hold on hard to stand both against the wind and against the water from a lot of sea which was coming across the foredeck. However, the job was easy enough and the only damage was a wooden batten snapped in three parts by the flogging main as it was coming down.

I topped up Miranda and lit Tilley to lend a light of cheer and compete with the lightning. There was not much else I could do, so when each deluge, which sounded like big hail stones, hitting the deck, started I slid off below. After watching for two hours I took off my oilskins and lay down in my clothes. But it was difficult to rest because of the racket not from the storms because I scarcely heard the thunder above the row in the ship, everything clashing and banging as she rolled, with seas from all directions thumping the ship.

I found the moon shining in at 0350 and went up to re-hoist the main although I had resolved not to do anything of the sort till dawn. But I found a huge storm ahead, in spite of a patch of clear sky around the moon so I returned to roost. Then of course I did sleep, overslept the dawn and did not resurface till 0630.

Although it was disappointing to lose all those hours (eight hours) of fast sailing, it was not a total loss because in the period we went 38 miles under the jib only; an average speed of 4¾ knots. And in the right direction too, except for a few wanderings off in the storms. Once for example we headed off 60° to east of north for a few minutes to return to 315° in due course.

When I changed tacks after breakfast this morning and went up on deck two hours later I found we had only done 4 knots with a full mainsail set. I then checked the main sheet, which put up the log reading from 4·2 to 4·6 knots, then I resheeted the jib, which I had sheeted too far aft (dull-wit) and hardened it a lot afterwards. This put up the reading from 4·6 to 5·6 knots.

153

That's where a yacht properly raced with a good crew would gain enormously. A good helmsman would size all that up in a few seconds whereas I lost two hours of the extra speed. The same applies to the thunderstorms last night. With a crew you could raise and lower your main as often as you liked. In fact I don't suppose I would have lowered it until forced to.

It makes all the difference to have a good man at the helm who can luff up in a squall and let the foredeck hands lower the sail easily. In the same way it is no trouble hoisting the main with a helmsman to luff up at a sign, thus taking the load off the slides and easing the pressure of the sail against the mast or shrouds. Single-handed it is too risky to try because an unwanted tack at that moment causes horrible confusion.

Later – tut! tut! tut! this is not my clever day. I interrupted this to go and get my local noon latitude. I have given up trying to know an accurate time for longitude but am keen to get the noon shot when time is not a critical factor. It is nice and sunny out though the sea is getting roughish. I stood with one foot on the seat each side of the cockpit and balanced myself with my middle against the hatch. I was sighting the sun above the sail and the horizon beneath it. I thought it quite safe there for a few minutes in ordinary clothes. I caught a sea which dashed right into the cockpit and soused me to the skin, jersey, shirt, trousers, also the sextant, watch and notebook.

I decided that the only thing to do with the sextant was to put it under the fresh-water tap and thoroughly hose it with fresh water. Well, I must get weaving, work out the sun sight and get some radio beacon bearings with the Heron-Homer. Thank heavens that is working perfectly to date.

I'm back in the old situation, wind dead in the eye from New York. Both tacks make me unhappy. This southerly one is the better but it means passing close south of Sable Island instead of 50 miles north of it as I intended. Therefore I must navigate seriously. I hope that island I dread is not hypnotizing me like a snake drawing me to it. All the ships wrecked on it, as far as I can make out, have thought themselves well away to the east of it. There is

154

apparently a very powerful current setting westwards onto it at times.

1930 hrs. Do you think one of the leprechauns they left in the yacht when they built her at Arklow, Eire, has taken a dislike to me and is trying to stop me from reaching New York? This afternoon it blew up to Force 6 and, more important to me, with a very windy sky, torn-up cirrus or mare's tails in an otherwise fine sunny setting. It was too much for the poor mainsail so I lowered it and hoisted the trysail. That's all very well if only I could point to New York. With the sea running rough enough to make it hard to stand in the cabin, and the strong wind, as usual right in my eye looking towards New York, I can't get the boat to point better than 55° off on either tack.

I changed tacks again and am now headed to pass Sable Island on the mainland side. At least I should have 10 miles a day current to help. I suppose instead of grousing about today I ought to be grateful for a good day's sailing yesterday when the run was 131 miles in the right direction.

11th July. 1845 hrs. It has been a noisy afternoon with terrific slams from the seas. *Gipsy Moth* ought to have been a ski jumper; she rushes up the side of a wave and takes off at the top. Her favourite trick is to sidle up and as she takes off at the crest she goes over with a quick flick onto her side before she crashes down the other side of the wave.

Its odd about this solo sailing, one jogs along for hours, perhaps days – how shall I put it – feeling quite secure and then suddenly a vague apprehension creeps in and blights one's peace of mind like mildew. At the moment I am charging towards the Nova Scotia coast and a bearing I took of the Sable Island radio beacon put me 24 miles farther east than my dead reckoning worked up for 2¼ days.

A latitude I got from a sun sight puts the northing of the DR as correct. It just made me wonder what I would do if I were asleep in my berth thinking a coast 24 miles ahead when in fact it wasn't. I consider the Sable Island beacon is correct and if we continue on this present heading I shall expect to see Cranberry Isle light abeam at four o'clock tomorrow morning (if I'm awake, which I doubt).

I have just looked at the chart and find the light on the island is only visible twelve miles away and I expect we shall be twenty miles south of it. The last bit of land I saw was the Eddystone Rock and light house if you can call that land.

I keep on digressing. I wanted to tell you about that 24-mile discrepancy in the DR. As it is downwind-upwind I would think that either the current is checked by a steady sou-wester blowing against it for days on end — 2¼ days at 10 miles a day makes up the 24 miles — or what I think is more likely, that each tack against the wind is less good in the average than I assess it at.

For hours at a time especially at night I do not look at the steering compass and I assess the average heading by what I see before and after going below. The tell-tale is not compensated or swung and is up to 15° out on some headings.

I had a wonderful sleep last night due to the trysail, which, after much havering I left set for the night. With that sail set *Gipsy Moth* steals quietly through the night and I never have a qualm.

I kept it set all morning when I would not normally, while I renewed the topping lift tackle of the main boom. The rope was stretched thin and would not have lasted much longer. Also I thought one of the blocks was not man enough for the heavy strain so I renewed that. The shock-cord preventer had parted so I renewed that at the same time. This all took a lot of time with the splicing and whipping and rigging.

When at last I did hoist the main we went slower than with the trysail and with a most infernal banging and slamming, taking a lot of water aboard. After lunch I lowered the main and rolled in two reefs but I think I spent a good hour messing about with the trim of the sails, the tiller-lines and Miranda before the ship settled down to a nice speed, sails asleep instead of drumming, and the seas that came aboard reduced to a reasonable size. There is no doubt the rig with the mainsail set enables the ship to point much closer to the wind than with the trysail.

12th July. 0845 hrs. Do you suffer from lack of adventure?

If so, try closing the Nova Scotian shore after dark, not certain where you are, and run into dense fog, visibility 50 yards, laced with rain and plenty of wind.

When I left off talking to you last night, it all seemed so simple. I only had to carry on till I got a fix from one of the coastal lighthouses. And I felt my luck was in because at dinner (herring roes lightly fried in butter with new potatoes – at least they were new a while ago), *Gipsy Moth* did one of her fancy bronco bucks.

The swinging table is amazing. I can leave things such as a jug of water on it for a day but of course it cannot swing more than, I should say, 60° because then the swinging part hits the two feet or legs on which the table is built.

Gipsy M's little antic brought the table-top hard up against the legs. (I always sit to the side of the table because otherwise my knees would prevent its swinging to the full.) The impact of table against its support jumped a bottle of whisky off the table up into the air where it somersaulted and started falling to the cabin sole neck downwards. I caught it on the way down before it hit the cabin sole. That's why I thought my luck was in.

At 2215 hrs. we were enveloped in thick fog. I had dined pretty well and was looking forward to a good sleep before starting to keep a look-out for the land. Let's face it, charging into fog stuffed with a coast as rough as North Brittany is no joke.

I went over my navigation again and made out that I had 20 miles clear of land. Therefore I could carry on for two hours and have a much-needed sleep for that period. I lay down and dropped off to sleep.

The whole outfit began behaving like a thwarted spoilt boy. The jib began a thunderous drumming, the mainsail flapped, *Gipsy M.* jumped and bucked, pitched and rolled, and every time I dozed off a big sea crashed on the foredeck or against the hull and woke me. The wind set up a beastly high-pitched whine in the rigging; even Miranda was flapping wildly.

I wanted to keep on that heading because it was far nearer the heading required than the other tack would be. Also the forecaster had promised a southerly later and if I

157

,could only hold on till that came, I should hardly lose any distance as I must do if I tacked and ran south for the night.

But the rest of the ship's company was not having any such thing and at half-past midnight I could not stand the bedlam any longer, gave up trying to sleep, dressed, lit Tilley for the stern and tacked ship away from the land. On this other tack everything seemed to quieten down. I went below and slept hard till six o'clock.

When I came to plot the night's doings on the chart I found I had made a most stupid blunder the night before in my plotting. There were two charts on the chart table. The top one on which I was plotting had its left-hand margin turned down to make it fit on the chart table. The edge of the chart below was showing on the left and I had measured my distance off the coast from its latitude scale which was less than half the scale of the chart above. (This was all by candle light.) Therefore instead of being 20 miles from land I must have been only 8 off and when I tacked only 3. Therefore, had I gone into a deep sleep for two hours I might have had a rude awakening.

It seems to me that the rest of the equipage were determined I should not get to sleep till I had tacked and they all kicked up hell's delight until I did so; it does seem amazing to me that the whole ship was quiet again as soon as I had tacked away from the coast. I am recording plain unmistakeable facts. I do not try to explain them.

I tacked again at dawn and I am approaching the coast again (farther along of course) in fog of medium density. The radio beacon bearings, not only don't agree with my DR but are not agreeing with each other. Even if I had an accurate time, which I have tried hard to get with no success, I could not take a sun-shot because of the fog. Accurate time would have enabled me to get an accurate longitude yesterday which would have been a good basis for the night's dead reckoning. Oh, well, I have always thought the fascination of navigation is not so much getting a fix as getting yourself out of the other kind of fix when you are in it. So I must leave you and put the old skull cap on for a bit of intense guess-work.

1700 hrs. I just cannot understand it but I am accepting it; going back to July 9 there was a discrepancy between the DR and the fix by sun and radio bearing; the DR position was 23 miles due west of the fix. I accepted that and started the DR afresh. On the 11th, two days later there was another discrepancy of a similar amount 32 miles due west. I took no notice of this but carried on the DR plot started two days earlier. Another fix on the 11th at 1800 hrs. made it 25 miles west. At 0745 this morning a bearing from Sable Island made it 23 miles. At 1130 another Sable Island backed by one from Sambro light vessel now coming within reliable range made it 23. Now at 1625 I have just had three bearings of Sable Island, Sambro light vessel and E. Point (north-east point of Nova Scotia). Conditions for observing are perfect with a smooth sea and steady ship and all three bearings meet at one point. And this point is 22½ miles due east of the three-day-old DR plot fix. I must accept it. I wonder if it could be a current trick.

I am used to making mistakes but I can nearly always account for them. It's odd that the same error built up in two days running on the 8th to the 9th and the 9th to the 10th of July. Could the Labrador current have been strongly reversed for two or three days? It has always puzzled me about the many wrecks on Sable Island when the men concerned seem to have thought they were well clear of it.

I should not be surprised if they get very big and strong eddies occasionally caused by the Gulf Stream and the Labrador conflicting. The Labrador is accepted as a SW. half-knot average and the Gulf Stream a NE. half-knot up to 2 knots in the heart of it at these latitudes. It flows at 6 knots down south.

Now I am happy with my fixes and am charging forward as fast as possible headed for the land in dense fog. It is one of those dilemmas, this tack – we are hard on the wind as usual – is nearly good enough to clear Nova Scotia but not quite. But the longer I can carry on in this direction, the better, because the other tack will only take me away from the land at the cost of heading east of south.

At one period today we were just pointing sufficiently well to have cleared the land but it was nearly calm then, since when we have been slowly headed back to the north-west.

I must say I have fairly wallowed in the peace and quiet of today. As I was drinking my cup of tea this afternoon; what a contrast with tea-time yesterday when *Gipsy Moth*, practising her jumping, sent the jug of tea up into the air off the table. I couldn't help laughing, it seemed incredible that so many tea-leaves should come out of one spoonful of tea. They went not only over the table but over the settee opposite, right across the floor and the side of my settee below me was plastered with tea-leaves. The laugh was due to those that entered the aperture under my settee and lodged on the dustpan kept there.

It has been very muggy and hot today and I can almost believe I shall not need woollen underfugs and an oilstove in New York in July, though heat seemed incredible a day or two ago. I hear the announcer of Cape Breton talking of 80° F. ashore there now, which seems pretty odd only a few miles away. Still no chance of drying anything with the dense fog. I wonder if I shall get dry the jerseys and things I got wet passing the Eddystone Light, June 11th, before reaching New York. This afternoon I felt all my trousers and wore the pair which seemed the least damp, a pair of track pants.

Although there has appeared to be no wind at times we have ghosted along all day mostly over 4 knots. If one kept still on the yacht, i.e. did not rock it or disturb its trim in the water, I believe it would sail with only a towel set in a zephyr. Anyway a good excuse for me to have a lazy day lying down sleeping and reading instead of doing the twenty jobs I ought to do such as trying to mend the navigation lights.

Our run yesterday was 118 and today 110½. Total to the hour logged, 3,056.

Oh, dear! I suppose I must get to work again. I said this coast was like N. Brittany. It has certainly got as many off-lying rocks all the way along and it stretches a long way – more than 300 miles. At the moment I am about 95 miles E. of Halifax.

Each of these radio bearings has four corrections to be worked out and applied to it. That's not quite true, one, the coefficient 'A' for the hand-held compass used in the

160

15 Tying up at Staten Island for quarantine

16a   After crossing the finishing line

16b   Sunshine at last—sailing through New York

operation is a constant and so is the magnetic variation for the time being. Then there is the deviation of the compass according to the ship's heading and due to the magnetism in the ship, the engine, the 4¼-ton iron keel, etc. Lastly there is the quadrantal correction due to the radio waves being bent by the rigging on their way in. This varies according to the direction of the beacon relative to the ship's heading.

This is thirsty work and the sun would be over the yard-arm if it weren't for the fog. Anyway, it is six o'clock, which is the time for all good men and true to down a noggin.

13th July. 1045 hrs. Breakfast at last. I've been kept hard at it since 0600. In fact I might almost say before that because I had to get up at three o'clock and lower and furl the main. The ship was like a squawking kid. The genoa and main decided there was too much wind to suit them; they stopped the ship, banged, flogged, rattled, whistled.

There was not much wind, perhaps Force 5, with a lovely fine moonlight night and the fog cleared away. But together they were not going to budge. As soon as I had the main furled and left the Genny to it, she was as happy as could be, started off straight away with hardly a sound and pulled the ship along at 4¾ knots for the rest of the night.

At 0600 hrs. I got up to tack ship. Then I reefed the main and rehoisted it. It is a labour for Hercules that reefing by oneself. I started counting the number of times I went along the deck from the mast to the cockpit and back, crouched and forced to use a handgrip somewhere nearly the whole way; but after I had counted to nine trips I forgot to carry on.

Mind you, the reefed sail is a nice job. The previous time I reefed I tried the ordinary way of just rolling up the sail. It had a horrible crease or fold about three feet in from the leech.

While I was at the tiller there was a loud sigh and I looked up, startled, to see some enormous dorsal fins curving slowly down into the water. I didn't see them again but think they were the same kind as I saw on the Grand Banks.

As soon as I had got the main reefed and set I went below and started getting breakfast and making the coffee

161

when the hullaballoo started again. One would think the genny hated the mainsail. It was hard to stand up in the cabin, the bows burying themselves, the cockpit with 6 inches of water in it. I could see they would only create an increasing hell until I did something about it so I left the coffee on the table and handed the genny, replacing her with that hardy warrior No. 2.

Now it is fairly quiet with the sun streaming into the cabin from the cockpit. If there was not so much sea flying about I could dry out some things on deck. But it is no good. They will only get wetter. This chattering won't do; *navigare necessare est*, as I think Henry the Navigator said.

2045 hrs. I just can't understand it. I hear on the radio from Sidney, Cape Breton Island, from Halifax and this morning Boston came in range. They all talk of light winds or south-westerly 15-m.p.h., and temperatures mentioned are in the eighties. Here am I, only a few miles away with not a really fine day since I left England.

This afternoon it blew up to gale very quickly with thick fog and a horrible sea but no one says a word about it. It has been a day of frustration; I seem to have worked hard all day for nothing. Every sail change has been wrong an hour later.

I was within a few miles of Halifax this afternoon and called them up on the R/T. Asked the operator to send a telegram to Chris Brasher of the *Observer*. I had difficulty in hearing him and had to ask him to repeat time after time. He had to ask me too. He got very suspicious. What was my call sign? Why hadn't I got any other channels?

I tried to explain that the GPO had taken out the crystals so that I couldn't use the other channels but it did sound pretty far-fetched put into words. Could he speak to the ship's radio operator? I tried to explain that there was no one else on board, but that sounded a bit queer too. 'Was this Lord Beaverbrook's yacht?' No, it wasn't; his son's *Drumbeat* had put into St John's to have a new mast fitted and had a crew of ten whereas this was a single-hander.

Then he said he couldn't hear me very well and suggested I should try somebody else. I said hastily that it didn't matter about the rest of the message if he would

162

send off what I had already given him. I said, 'Check up with Cape Race, they sent a telegram off for me a few days ago.' I feel I have done my duty but my brush with civilization made me feel jaded.

Soon after I tacked to the south again as I was getting near Halifax harbour entrance and I did not want to be in a steamer lane after dark in the thick fog. I have been sailing along this coast of Nova Scotia and Breton Isle for 150 miles off and on and have not seen a sign of it. It will be odd if I get to New York without seeing any land since Eddystone Rock.

When I turned away from Halifax I began making everything snug for what looked like a really dirty night. I dismantled the R/T aerial because it was chafing the reefed mainsail badly. After I had dealt with everything, the jib and reefed main were making such frightful heavy weather of it that I started putting my oilskins back on to set the trysail and hope for a night's peace. As I was dressing the wind lulled as quickly as it had blown up.

It is now so quiet that more sail seems needed. But I am not to be drawn. No more sail to be added till dawn. One takes life much too seriously.

I got quietly ticked off by the Primus stove, which for some days had burnt more and more feebly. I wondered if I could do anything about it and fiddled with it, cleaned it. Looking down from above, the two top pieces having been removed, I tried the turn-on knob and got a strong jet of paraffin straight in my eye. Wearing glasses I was all right, but I took it as a strong hint not to be so serious.

CHAPTER TWELVE

July 14th to 21st

Free Wind at Last – The Ship in the Fog – Promise of
Gale – Under the Storm Jib – School of Porpoises –
Mother Carey's Chickens and Mollyhawks – A Perfect
Sailing Day – The First Dry Patches – Starlit Night –
Tide Rip on George's Bank – Overcrowded Sea – Fish-
ing Smacks – The *Nicolas Bowater* – New York on
the Chart – Radio Bearing of Cape Cod – Nantucket
Shoal – Thick Fog and Flat Calm – The Sound of
Texas Tower – The Lurking Motor Vessel – 'Wonder-
ful Day at Sea' – The Forty Days in Danger! – The
First Land Sighted Since the Eddystone: Block Island
– Cleaning and Washing – Along Long Island – Talk-
ing to New York Coastguard – The ETA at Ambrose
Light – Becalmed – 'Your Wife is on Board' – You
Are First!'

14th July. 1055 hrs. It isn't rational; here am I biting my
mental fingernails through frustration and yet if I arrived
and returned to a city life I should be thinking of such a
jaunt as this all the time and wishing I were away on it.

The wind I have longed for is here this morning. It has
freed at last, a north-wester. Unfortunately it is younger
sister to a dead calm and besides advancing me only
2 miles in an hour and a half, it causes about five times as
much work as a sailing breeze. At least we are headed in
the right direction even if only at 1⅓ knots.

I saw a ship this morning so have visual evidence that
there is someone else on this planet. It seemed to be headed
for me in the fog, sounding its foghorn and I uneasily got
out my little tooter and a loaded Very pistol. It crossed my
bows and I saw its ghostly outlines through the fog.

15th July. 1115 hrs. I got myself out of a bagful of toil and trouble by a bit of canny laziness; never a dull moment! But wait a minute and I'll tell you of yesterday while a pot of Guinness sends its humanizing tentacles through my desiccated arteries – I've been in oilskins since six o'clock this morning.

I glibly say 'Never a dull moment' but yesterday was terrible. I didn't write any more, I was so low-spirited. Nothing does down a racing man (sorry, I had to make a dash for the tiller when we gybed. I'm afraid Miranda hasn't yet learnt properly what a gybe is) than a calm. Apart from being stuck, that awful slatting of sails and banging of blocks and tapping of halliards gets one down. And then the work is far more than in an honest straightforward gale; lowering and hoisting sails, changing sails and trim.

Finally at 2330 hrs. last night I gave up trying to make use of the faint puffs which kept on tantalizing all day. I lowered and furled the main, lowered the genoa and tied it down to the foredeck. If I went on trying to sail, the best result would only be a mile or two advanced during the night and me too dog tired if a real wind arrived next day to take advantage of it.

At 0400 hrs. I felt a breeze, so rousted myself out of my berth. I tried to make a cup of coffee but the Primus jibbed. I went on deck and began unfurling the main. Then I thought 'I'll make sure first what this wind is.' I had poked my head up and assessed it at north. Now, certainly, it was north-east. That meant, no mainsail but twin spinnakers with booms fully rigged. That was a man-size job especially in the dark and I decided the Primus must work and I must have some coffee before I set about it. This was when, after a second cup and some breakfast, my canny laziness took charge and I decided to return to my blankets and sleep till dawn.

At the back of my mind must have been the big smooth swell which had begun creeping in from the south yesterday afternoon. That meant a storm somewhere even if the surface of the swell was oily calm. I woke at six to find a Force 7 wind in full whine with promise of a vicious little gale.

I thanked my stars that I had not been caught out with all that spinnaker nonsense with the terrific to-do of rigging it all first and then double the effort to get it all in in a gale two hours later. However, a real north-easter was too good to miss so I hopped up as quickly as I could and after bagging the genoa and making the loosely furled main snug I set the little storm jib and did the best I could to set the ship running before the wind.

Unfortunately running puts a heavy load on the rudder and as Miranda has to have her spanker topped-up to avoid fouling the backstay she has not enough power to control the rudder. So we wander downhill between south and west with an occasional gybe to north of west which requires my darting up to put the helm over and bring her back to south of west.

After a second breakfast I set the trysail. While doing so I watched a vast school of porpoises. They were near but not taking any notice of *Gipsy Moth* unless *Gipsy Moth* was making them surface.

As soon as I set the trysail the ship became quiet and seemed to amble or sidle quietly downwind. From the cabin I could clearly hear, quite far off, the hiss of the combers as they came up astern. They are not very big and yet it is amazing in how short a time they build up from a calm sea. Now I can hear the hiss of heavy rain on the sea as well as on the deck.

I wish this blow would last two days and put me well south. I wouldn't mind being pushed into the Gulf Stream because it ought to be followed by a northerly which would give me a free wind to make straight for New York.

1605 hrs. What a vast difference between running before a gale and bashing into it. I was in the cockpit watching Miranda's handiwork and could not tear myself away for an hour . . . the keynote of the blow seems a big deep sigh. If one is fussy and listens to the detail the whine and occasional shriek of the wind are there. Of course the cockpit is a very sheltered spot with the dodgers rigged at the sides.

The Mother Carey's Chickens whom I dread seeing in fine weather because bad nearly always follows after you have seen them, look wonderful skimming the surface. They seem very intrigued by the log-line which I see snaking its way over the waves and from side to side like a piece of loose string dropped wriggling on the floor. One would think the log rotator would pull it out straight and would find it difficult to follow such a tortuous path. I saw one Mother C's Chicken peck at the line. There are bigger birds, Mollyhawks I guess, which seem to be enjoying themselves zooming up into the blast.

I was watching to see if the combers would poop us. It has always been said that the disturbance of the water by a ship causes the waves to break. This boat has such a clean design of hull that she scarcely disturbs the water as she slips through at 5 knots.

The fog has gone, thank heaven! I'm glad to get away from Nova Scotia. I coasted it for 150 miles, I suppose, without a glimpse because of the fog. I've got the stove going again, though, it is so chilly and clammy in the cabin.

16 July. 0835 hrs. Well, here it is at last! The perfect sailing day. Broad reach to a north wind Force 3. Not a cloud in the sky. Big round sun. Small crescent moon (waning).

It looks as if I might even dry out some of my things. My rope-soled shoes had better go overboard. Though they have remained under the dining-room table they are covered with mildew. However, if the day stays like it is I shall have to hunt around for something else to moan about.

Last night, from a racing viewpoint, I did an awful thing. I knew I was wasting miles by not setting more sail during the night but I went on strike and turned over under the blankets. Everything in the ship was kicking up the most frightful cacophony: jam jars clashing, kettles sliding across the floor, table-flap banging loudly, Primus banging the toaster on the side because it was swinging so hard: add all this to the slapping of wire sheets on the deck, wire runners against the dinghy, and halliards against the mast, chuck in the violent jerks and abrupt rolls and you have the mixture for bedlam. What did I do? Turned over and went to sleep again.

Last evening it was blowing hard Force 7 and though we were running fast Miranda was not strong enough to control the rudder. The following seas picked up the stern and slewed it to one side or the other. It was as much as I could do at times to man-handle the rudder to get back on course, so how could a topped-up Miranda cope?

I was not going to stay up at the helm all night, though
167

I could not resist remaining for an hour, it was such good sport. And impressive too! Looking down from the stern when on top of a wave the seas looked a good size for the short time it had been blowing. They rolled down onto the stern from on high and just as I thought we were going to be pooped, the stern rose and let the sea slide under as if it were a duck pond matter.

I thought hard for a while because I was in the old fix the windjammers dreaded, though for a different reason; I had run too long. I couldn't leave the tiller to tend the sheets of the trysail. After thinking and waiting for half an hour an opportunity came when the seas let the ship alone for a brief period but long enough for me to hop on the stern and release Miranda whom I had been over-riding all this time. Then I hardened in the spitfire jib and slacked away the trysail halliard a little before a thunderous gybe brought me scuttling back to the tiller. With a number of such trips to the mast I got the trysail down and secured.

The ship's movement eased at once and Miranda took control with ease. And so I left her with only the spitfire storm jib set. The speed went down to 3 knots but it meant peace and sleep. In the middle of the night the wind eased and I could have set sail but I slept on. I think it cost me 10 miles but I slept on.

2130 hrs. I saw the horizon cut the sun in half and then the sun sank slowly into the sea. It was gone. No, that was only a swell over it. But now it has gone for good. All round the horizon the sky had a roseate tint. Not a cloud in the sky. And we amble smoothly along. This is what makes one love sailing.

But what a day! You would scarcely recognize this ship. There are patches dry on the cabin sole; there are damp streaks where the floorboards meet but even one dry patch is an event after a month.

I've been bustling about all day. A stream of things, clothes, bedding, mattresses, cushions being hustled on deck. Later when dry, brushing off the mildew. Hatches open, ventilators reversed to send the air down in a strong stream. We have been sailing on all day even if only slowly. The wind has gradually headed us off, until now we are pointing at 200° compass, far beyond where I would have tacked normally as our proper course is 276°.

The US Weather Bureau forecaster says we shall have a northerly tomorrow and so far his predictions have all been right. It's the sou-wester I expect after that, that worries me. I don't want to be caught close inshore and have to head off east of south. However, the time to tack has arrived.

17th July. 0835 hrs. St John's time. Last night a bright starlit night. I was enchanted, the first clear bright starry sky I have seen for months. The stars had that diamond sparkle I associate with a frosty December night.

I was not surprised to be called out at 0130 for a she-mozzle. This is what happens: a lull of calm; a wave gives the rudder a buffet and it swings to one side. Miranda windless is powerless. Having gone 20° the rudder wallops hard over, dragging Miranda by the tiller-lines. The yacht has enough way on to come up into the wind. The genoa is backed against the shrouds. Now back comes a puff of wind. The genny is backed really hard against the shrouds. Miranda is locked hard over. She is only designed to work the tiller through a 30° arc and once outside that she gets locked in a position impossible to escape from. Though for that matter, no amount of rudder will overcome a big head-sail aback.

My drill is first to let the runner go which the boom is hard against, then release Miranda, next let the genoa's sheet fly, haul in the genoa's other sheet and proceed to tack normally. I think it is the devil of a job in a near calm with faint puffs and in the dark and I made several bosh shots before succeeding. I must take both runners up to the mast next time before starting. Those four lethal blocks flying round in the dark take a bit of watching, and by the time I have nipped aft onto the stern to clock in Miranda, the genoa is aback again the other side and the whole drill has to be repeated.

I got a pleasant surprise, however, because when I finally turned in again, expecting to be called out again at any moment there was not another murmur from my crew and I slept peacefully till six while they slaved away faithfully in the dark.

At six I woke to dense fog. That marvellous day yesterday made me think the fog was finished. At least there was a good breeze with it and I darted out bare-legged into the cockpit for a quick preliminary fiddle with the trimming.

I found that we have sailed into a tide rip. There was no mistaking those short steep seas with breaking crests. I thought we must be in a shoal but I could not remember anything to indicate it on last night's chart. When I could go below to study the chart I found that we had just passed over a kind of canyon a thousand fathoms deep running NE. to SW. and had just crossed the George's Bank side of it into only 85 fathoms. It looks like a nearly vertical wall of 5,000 feet below us just there.

I still don't understand the tide rip because a look at the tide tables indicated a tide current against us at that moment of 1·9 knots flowing off the bank into the canyon. Perhaps there is a vertical eddy there like the air updraught in the lee of a range of mountains. Anyway it was a surprise for me thinking myself out in the Atlantic. One tends to associate tide rips with places like the Needles Channel.

Into this canyon runs a branch which must have drained the Gulf of Maine and Bay of Fundy. This is a mere 110 to 150 fathoms deep.

I'm sorry, I was wrong; another look at the chart shows it was not a canyon but a vast wall or cliff. Where we crossed it the bottom rises from 1,000 to 100 fathoms within 4½ miles. If there is a rip like that on the edge of the bank I must look up in the 'Admiralty Pilot for the USA East Coast' to see what it says about the 2-fathom shoal in the centre of George's Bank. Here it is: 'This part (the shallow part) should be avoided; in heavy weather the sea breaks in patches with depths of 10 fathoms or less, and strong tide rips are encountered, the latter, however, not always indicating shoal water.' It goes on to describe the Nantucket Shoals which come after George's Bank. Cheerful words, 'These shoals extend 40 miles south-eastward of Sankaty Head lighthouse . . . and render this one of the most dangerous parts of the US coast.'

The sea is fairly rough here. I would have thought it would be calm because we are on the lee side of George's Bank and should get shelter from it. Now we are embarked on this tack I think we had better carry on round the George's Shoal keeping to the north of it which is after all the lee side. Then tack again 'in about a day's time to pass between George's Shoal and Nantucket Shoals.

I must do some navigating, get a fix off the USA radio beacons if possible. I like to get used to them in good time. They all have a distinctive note of their own which usually identifies them without need of the call letter once you are used to them. For instance Western Head Nova Scotia has a yelp like a quiet puppy.

1820 hrs. New York time. The sea is getting overcrowded. This afternoon I passed a fishing smack called *Cobalt* (I think) and saw two others in the distance. The Pilot says one can expect lots on these shoals.

Just now I was concentrating on a most important job below: I had been presented with a cardboard carton in Plymouth labelled 'Survival Kit to be opened only if lost or on arrival USA'. It had been presented by Coates, makers of Plymouth Gin so I had a shrewd idea what was in it. As I had finished off my whisky and gin the day before yesterday, you can imagine how I had been eyeing this package ever since. I considered George's Bank could be called USA and that I could at last open up the package. Inside, oh frabjous joy! was a bottle of the famous gin. I filled in a form they enclosed, giving details of the position, time, etc. and threw it overboard as requested in a bottle which they offer to exchange for a bottle of gin if found.

I was opening up the gin when suddenly I heard voices. I thought, 'Good God! Am I too late?'

I popped my head out into the cockpit and there were the voices. The *Nicolas Bowater*, London, was close by on its way back along my route and five people were sitting up on the boat-deck having their evening cocktail. I wonder what they thought seeing a yacht with apparently no one on board.

Grog, by the way is essential medicine for solo Atlantic races; not only does it keep the scurvy away, if mixed with lemon juice, but mental scurvy as well.

Do you know I can feel a teeny weeny little bit of excitement budding. My present chart has New York on it. I'm still on George's Bank but after crossing a channel come the Nantucket Shoals and after that a run along Long Island to New York. It was quite a thrill this morning to get a radio bearing of Cape Cod which has always seemed such a romantic spot. This afternoon I got my fix off Nantucket Light Vessel, Pollock Rip, Cape Cod, and Halfway Rock (Portland N.H.). I used Seal Island for a check (at the tail end of Nova Scotia).

What a race! Here I am after sailing 3,516¼ miles, not knowing how I am placed. How well I know that heartsink on finding one's rivals waiting. But even if I were last I would still have that feeling which it gives you to have sailed a route like this. I hope I don't see any buoys as I thread the Nantucket Shoals (which I expect to do); I do hope the Ambrose Light can be the first landmark to see since the Eddystone.

Gipsy Moth is beetling along as if she too wants to get in. We are in another tide rip and a lot of spray is coming aboard but I risked popping out without oilskins to see the log, 6¼ knots, distance 3,524.

I must have a good study of the chart to see if I can sleep in peace tonight. At a critical time I have to tack to move south between George's and Nantucket Shoals, then turn as soon as we reach the first practical passage through the Nantucket labyrinth.

The weather forecast is good. The US Weather Bureau forecaster at Boston predicts a sw. along Long Island and a northerly in the north portion of his territory. I think he refers to the New England States but where does the northern portion begin? A northerly for me when I want to move south between George's and Nantucket would be a big stroke of luck. At present we are hard on the wind and as usual headed too far north.

18th July. 1830 hrs. For once we are nearly headed where we want to go. We amble along at 4½ knots. Sometimes in the cabin I think we are becalmed, it becomes so quiet; I go on deck to find we are still doing the 4½ knots. It has been a sunny, fine day too. What more could one wish for?

You know how it is near the end of a voyage; the seeds of discontent are sown. Last night I slept badly. First, I find

172

it hard sometimes to relax and disregard a kind of blind or trapped feeling at pressing on into the dark while I go to sleep; secondly I was excited by the thought of the race nearing its end.

Today I dampened some of the romance of this voyage by trying to contact land by R/T. They could not hear me well enough, could not hear what I said. Why do I spoil the peace by trying? Well, Sheila is waiting in New York and it seems mean not to let her know I am on the way.

The interesting problem for me is the Nantucket Shoal, which I am headed for. From the chart I can't see anything against threading my way through and it will save 10–20 miles if the wind is free to New York on the other side. I only worry about being becalmed if Nantucket Island is a hot sandy place. Also it would be bad tactics to enter the labyrinth of shoals against the tide current. The current will be favourable there at 0900 hrs. tomorrow which is roughly when we should be there. I must not risk being stuck in there especially if the current, up to nearly 2 knots, is contrary. I had better get my evening fix before the twilight distorts the radio waves.

19th July. 1105 hrs. That was a night; rather exciting really. I've just sat down to breakfast so it was a pretty lengthy night too. I had a good sleep from 2300 hrs. to 0115 hrs., when I got up for a radio beacon fix, and I slept soundly again for another hour and a quarter till 0315.

I woke up with a start and remembered we were heading for the middle of Nantucket shoals and I must do something about it. There were no lights to get bearings from, I could not get depth soundings which are so valuable for navigation and radio bearings are apt to be capricious at night.

As if to accentuate my blind approach to the Shoals the night was as black as pitch though it appeared quite fine. The only thing to do was to get sets of radio beacon bearings at intervals, run up the DR alongside regardless of the radio results and act in a way that would be safe and effective whichever was right.

None of these radio bearing fixes agreed with each other, and the DR differed from them all.

173

If one has accurate, reliable information to work on it seems to me that navigation is a simple science, but it is when one has to deduce the right results from uncertain information that navigation becomes an art. It is then that it has its great fascination.

I worked out that I could go through the Shoals on one heading, which would take me through safely no matter which of the fixes was right and which was wrong. Suspense and excitement were considerable, and heightened, although I don't think they ought to have been, by the fact that the last landmark or seamark which I had seen was the Eddystone Rock, 3,700 miles of sailing earlier.

Luck was with me because the wind was backing steadily which enabled me to enter the Shoals at a suitable place without having to tack south-east first. At 0500 hrs. the sky began to brighten and I could see a squall of at least rain ahead so hurriedly put on a full kit of oilskins. When it reached us I downed the mainsail. It turned into a big thunderstorm with lashings of heavy rain.

I passed over one shoal. I could hear it rustling – a very uncanny sound – but I was not frightened of this one because there was sufficient depth over it. It was impressive to see the sea gathering as if to break. The danger of these shoals is that one breaking swell will dump the yacht on the sandbank, and the next will founder it.

My track would take me or should take me by my reckoning within a mile or two of what the chart called a 'Texas Tower, floodlit' so I expected to see a landmark at last. But it was not to be. Thick fog rolled up. Presently I could hear the Tower, a foghorn giving two deep 'moos' like a sick bull. On the port bow where it should be. But, if the wind squall, the thunder storm, the deluge and the fog were not enough, now it fell calm. And still is.

I am not happy stuck in the middle of this maze of shoals and sandbanks and I have been working like a beaver all the morning. Unfortunately I cannot get a good fix because all the most valuable radio beacons, Cape Cod, Pollock Rip and Nantucket light vessel, are in a line from here so that they are only worth one position-line instead of a cross of several giving a fix.

Some other beacons to the west which I have tried to use

174

to get a cut are either too far away or have land between them and here, in either case making them unreliable. However, I kept on taking bearings all the same, and I formed a picture of where I was.

I've got the ghoster genoa set and have been nursing it, humouring its every whim all morning. It does keep the boat moving even when there is not enough wind to blow cigarette smoke away. My best tack is heading us for some serious shoals but I am reckoning that the current combined with our movement results in pressing us out slowly to the westward.

I can only carry on this caper for another hour and a half till 1620 hrs. If the situation does not change for the better I shall have to roust out the kedge and anchor where we are. Otherwise with the current turned and flowing at 2 knots (at its strongest) we shall be carried into the thick of the maze. However, God tempers the wind, etc. and if we have a calm at least it is then possible (I hope) to drop a kedge. Well we'll see; a lot can happen in an hour and a half on this voyage.

Meanwhile lunch before I get involved in a spate of action. I must say I have been pretty busy since 0315; twelve hours in fact, but it is rather sport (provided we can get out of this sand trap).

PS. I must tell you one little joke. I was bustling in the cockpit when I turned round startled. A cloud of steam had enveloped me. You must admit a bit of a surprise out here. Of course you know the answer: some dense white fog. It seems to indicate a finger of the Gulf Stream feeling its way in here where it should not be. Reserved for the Labrador current, this alley way.

1700 hrs. Well, would you believe it? I could scarcely tear myself away from the deck scene it is so fascinating – only that I gave Miranda a tap and the radar reflector she has to carry, poor dear, disgorged half a pint of fog-drops from the meshwork and soaked my shirt to the skin.

I had my lunch, my usual potatoes and onions with Cohoe salmon and Bartlett pears to follow. I washed up too like a dutiful househusband. Then I fished out the lead and line to plumb the depths before dropping the kedge. No sense in dropping an anchor into a bottomless hole.

When I got on deck we were moving nearly as fast as the tide would be flowing. And there, like a hungry wolf snapping at our heels, was a tide rip like a hundred potato rows on a larger scale. Row after row, quite even, with the crest combing here and there. Just before they reached the counter of the yacht they stopped completely and the sea round us was smooth, quite smooth with humpy seas beginning to form as it were under smooth skin. These looked as breakers do humping themselves up gathering their bulk before combing and breaking.

I turned round to see if any were in fact breaking ahead of us but there were none. So I hoisted the mainsail. I thought if we can go this speed with the genoa only maybe we can beat the tide with the mainsail added. Try it anyhow. We are doing more than 2 knots but we are crossing the lines of shoals and crossing the direction of the tide. So, although we may be going faster than 2 knots the tide is still carrying us into the shoals at 2 knots sideways to our direction of movement. I don't want to get caught in a bad position and find the wind petering out (as I fear it is doing at the moment).

1745 hrs. We are still moving but I am not happy. We have 20 miles of this stuff to cross yet. It is a question of whether we can avoid being caried too far in during the six hours of tide setting in that direction. It seems curious that with all this current the actual rise and fall of the tide is very little here, about 13 inches maximum. Well, I'll have a siesta (I'm certainly due one) and maybe I'll get an inspiration.

20th July. 0040 hrs. That last move of mine was a good one. When I resurfaced at ten past nine after my snooze, I found the ship going well. Miranda must have called a conference after I left and they decided to show what could be done if only I would leave them alone. Master Ghoster was pulling really well and they were doing 5 knots.

We were lucky to get away from that place. On the way out we were sailing through one of the tide rips and only just gaining on it. For quite a time the stern of the boat was in the tide rip and the bows were in smooth-surfaced water. Since we emerged in the dark we have twice been way-

176

laid by a motor vessel. I watched it while it waited for us to come up to it. When we were close it crossed our bows – too close for my comfort; one never knows what these powered vessels know about yachts and I had no navigation lights so he could claim he thought me stationary if he hit me. After that he sheered off but he or another similar turned up again an hour later. Are they coastguards (but don't you think they would speak to me if they were?) or do you think they were considering hi-jacking me or whatever they do now in American thrillers? I must stop because my eyes refuse to stay open.

1915 hrs. It's not racing but it has been a wonderful sail, or should I put it better as 'a wonderful day at sea'? It was hot enough to lunch in the cockpit stripped for a sunbath. That was wonderful after the past month. But from a racing point of view I've had to pay for it by having thick fog during the night and half the morning and a very light wind this afternoon dead in the eye from New York as usual. So we have been ambling along at 1–2 knots. Bang goes my chance of finishing tomorrow morning, which would have made the crossing forty days.

Suddenly becalmed, I had to go and sort out the schemozzle. I hope it is for a wind-shift to the north-west as promised by the forecaster. Yesterday he said it would be southerly to sou-westerly today and I ambled off all the afternoon on the southerly tack in anticipation of this southerly wind coming. But it has been the usual wnw. all day.

When I started this race I had high-flying ambitions of finishing in four weeks; then I had hoped for thirty days. Now forty days is going west. I suppose I shall find the rivals who have gone by the Azores south route will all be in New York.

I sighted my first land or landmark today since the Eddystone. It was Block Island at the entrance to Long Island Sound. I was sorry in a way because I thought it would have been amusing not to sight anything between Eddystone and the Ambrose light vessel.

Sighting land does make navigation easy, it was only necessary to take off the bearings of the two ends of the island to get a fix in a minute instead of waiting for radio beacons to start their signals, then get the bearings, in fact lots of bearings usually.

I have worked like a beaver all day . . . cleaning and washing the cabin, the stove, everything . . . shave, hair cut, washing shirts. Sheila dropped me a pretty broad hint I think when she said it was quite unnecessary for a single-handed voyager to turn up looking like a tramp with a filthy boat. She is right, too. But still a little sordid squalor is rather nice sometimes when the alternative is hard labour with brushes and things.

I quite understand why people used to – and still do – go into retreat. During a month alone I think at least you become a real person and you are concerned only with the real values of life.

21st July. 0020 hrs. What a disappointment! When the wind came it was a northerly instead of southerly and gave us a broad reach. We fairly scuttled along at 7¼ knots for an hour and a half. I got quite excited at the possibility of a good romp to the finishing line.

But it was not to be; the wind has just backed to north-west and we are hard on the wind again. You would think, wouldn't you, that in a 4,000-mile race we might have had a good fast reach for one day.

It was rather a crisis when the wind stole upon us out of the calm. I set Miranda and clamped her to the tiller-lines, then started hoisting the mainsail. But I had it half up when it fouled the confounded R/T aerial. So I had to lower it and partly lower the aerial to get that out of the way.

I had the main half hoisted again, when I suddenly noticed that Miranda was not in the attitude I expected. I had to drop the main right down again and bustled aft to the stern. I found Miranda's clamp was not working. This was a serious matter. If anything happened to M, I should be in a bad way . . . I dismantled the clamp and found a spindle was rusted in.

This was soon put right. What a relief! Up went the main and we were off. A wonderful thing, going fast at night. Can't keep awake. Good night. Good night.

0400 hrs. Still at it. I never got that sleep I mentioned. We were off course and by the time I had checked sheets of both genoa and mainsail and retrimmed all round something else had cropped up. I don't mind; it is pretty exhilarating to be charging through a starlit night at 7·1 knots, which is what we have averaged since 2300 hrs. A broad reach which we are back to is the most difficult to trim for self-steering to keep a steady course within a few degrees. Normally, with sea room I wouldn't mind Miranda ranging over an arc of 30 or 40° on a broad reach but here we are sailing along the 100-mile straight front of Long Island and a change of course while I slept could soon have us charging up the beach at this speed.

Though there are lights (marine and air) along the island you can only see one at a time, which makes it hard work – longer work. I've just done a thing I don't approve of unless there is nothing better, taken a running fix of an airport beacon. I rough-checked the result with two radio beacon bearings. None of all these is reliable on its own in the night but they form a picture. I'm trying to keep a certain distance from the coast, 8 miles, to be just outside the steamer lane close inshore. I've seen quite a number of steamers pass.

63 miles to go at 0330: I wonder if this wind will hold.

0930 hrs. I made contact with a New York coastguard on the R/T and I am standing by the set at the moment expecting him to call me back after speaking to Ambrose Light. I had a wonderful sail last night – 64 miles in 9¾ hours. On the strength of it I told the coastguard I would be at Ambrose at 1330 if the wind holds. I fear it must drop however.

It is a day of days ... fine, cloudless, sparkling, calm-enough sea, nice sailing wind – the yachtsman's dream. 24 miles to go. What do you think? Will that black-bearded Viking be in already? I wish this coastguard would call me. I want to get on with my ship's husbandry (I had to sign the registration papers for the yacht as the 'ship's husband').

1050. Becalmed. Set ghoster. Lowered main. 3,979 miles (3,919 on log plus 60 unlogged at start and during voyage).

1143 hrs. Faint breeze. Started moving under ghoster only. Hard at it tidying decks and cabin. Very disappointed that I cannot possibly arrive at 1330 when I said I would if

179

the wind held. Cannot get contact on R/T with New York coastguards. Hoped a fishing-launch would approach so that I could ask it to R/T New York coastguards.

1330. Decided to have some lunch when the faint breeze livened up and I decided it was worthwhile setting the main.

I never got my lunch till twelve and a half hours later, two hours after the following midnight. From this moment everthing was excitement and action.

As soon as we began to move seriously I tried again to call up the New York coastguards. Suddenly a clear voice broke in which I could hear plainly. 'This is the *Edith G* at the Ambrose Light. Your wife is on board and wants to speak to you. I was surprised at this voice. I knew it but couldn't place it. (No wonder! It was Captain Percy, senior captain of BOAC – a fellow court member of the Guild of Air Pilots and Air Navigators who had been sent by the Grand Master, Prince Philip, and the Master K.G. Bergin, to welcome me on arrival. The last time I had heard his voice was at a court meeting of the Guild in London.)

He said: 'Your wife wants to speak to you.' I could hear a word or two from her but she was pressing the wrong button. Then Percy came on, strong-voiced: 'We will meet you . . . What is your course?' – '270°.' 'O.K. Two-seven-zero,' he said.

From now on, of course, my lunch was off. I watched every launch near by. I was now out of sight of land and it felt wrong to have left Fire Island to head out to sea again. I took another set of bearings from Ambrose, Barnegat and Fire Island to check my position. At 1550 I was met by a fishing-boat with my wife aboard looking very smart in her Mirman hat and friends waving greetings.

As soon as I could decently do so, I called out, 'Any news of the others?' The reply was honeysweet, 'You are first.'

But I was not to cross the finishing line all that easily. The wind veered and freshened. I had to down the ghoster and set old No. 2, the old warrior. Then I had a snappy beat to windward to reach the light vessel.

At 1730 I rounded the light vessel. The race was over 40 days 12 hours 30 minutes after the starting-gun. Distance sailed 4,004½ miles.

EPILOGUE

My voyage turned out wholly different from what I'd expected. For example I only expected a ration of one gale for the whole trip. And although I had considered the 10% probability of fog over 1,600 miles, I never expected that I would, in fact, sail through 1,400 miles of it equal to 2⅓ Fastnet races through continuous fog.

I certainly never expected to have headwinds for 2,600 miles of sailing. I was hard on the wind tacking all that distance which is foul sailing in Atlantic seas.

I think my yacht is too big for single-handed racing. The sails and booms are too big to handle in rough weather. The mainsail and genoa are each 380 square feet and, as previously stated, the yacht is nearly 40 feet long overall with a mast 55 feet high.

For solo *cruising* with smaller sails set it is not too big. If another solo transatlantic race took place and handicapping was asked for I would agree happily provided I was given a handicap for having too large a boat. A 9-tonner is the ideal size, in my opinion. All the same, I consider the idea of a non-handicap race a good one. And if the race is to do good for yachting, and I am quite certain it has already done so, then avoid handicaps. The value of the race is to find out the fastest ocean cruiser racer which one man can handle. If one man can handle it, then it must be all that easier for a crew to sail. In order that a big yacht can be sailed solo, devices and techniques for self-steering and easy handling must be perfected which will benefit yachting in general.

Miranda, my self-steering vane worked well – by the end of the race very well. By that time I'd learned a great deal more about sailing and could achieve much more from the trimming of the sails and of Miranda.

My rivals had much simpler and smaller vanes. With a rudder outside the transom of the boat, a tab rudder can be fitted to the trailing edge rather like the trimming tab at the trailing edge of the rudder of an aeroplane. It needs only a small vane which is a great advantage. Curiously the tab works in the opposite sense to the rudder. That is to say if you want your rudder moved to starboard the tab is moved to port and the pressure on the tab pushes the main rudder over to the other side. I think it might well result from this race that self-steering devices will become readily available for yachts. Personally I believe that I shall never try to cruise again without one. It means that two, say a man and wife, can cruise comfortably night and day with a self-steering device, and live a very pleasant life instead of being bound one or the other to the helm all the time. It's been said that when the Hiscocks sailed round the world they hardly ever met at sea because one was always on the helm, and the other asleep.

Here is what happened to some of my rivals. Blondie has only one sail on *Jester*, a kind of Chinese lug sail, which rolls down like a blind. His great success with this boat in his 48½-day crossing proves there must be something in his rig which might be going to revolutionize yachting. His theory is that yachting today is in the same state as would be automobile driving if every time you came to a hill you had to stop, jack up the back axle and change the back wheels for smaller ones in order to get uphill. According to the Met. charts, which I obtained after the race, he had similar weather to me except that he dodged my big storm.

The first three days he had the same gales that we all had, and he dropped behind the conventional-rigged boat. He went as far in three days as I went in the first two.

Later, bearing away northward from the headwinds must have paid him in extra speed, I suppose, and by July 1st he was ahead of me in longitude although 400 miles north.

At one point of his route he was only 300 miles from Greenland. Personally I think he made a mistake going up so far north, and that at the beginning of July he was in a poor position. He must come down southwards to get around Newfoundland, whether he wanted to or not. I think he lost time through that.

It would appear that he did not, by going far north, get into west-going circulation of depressions as he had hoped.

He gained particularly during the three days which I lost in the storm, but, although as I say he was ahead of me in

182

longitude, i.e. farther west on July 1st, by the time he reached Cape Race on July 14th, he was 6½ days behind me. After that, coming down the eastern seaboard of America he passed outside Sable Island and outside Nantucket light vessel. In other words his route was farther off the coast than mine. Blondie said he only took the helm for one hour between Europe and America but had to spend a lot of time adjusting his wind vane and steering apparatus to get his boat sailing right.

Blondie seems to have had an experience similar to my queer adventure off the Nova Scotia coast. In his case he was approaching the south-west corner of Ireland and, according to his dead reckoning, was well and truly in a safe position. He went below and turned in. Presently to his amazement the yacht tacked itself and went off on the other tack. He put his head up through his cubby hole to see what had gone wrong and a short distance away was the Irish coast with the waves breaking on the rocks.

David Lewis in *Cardinal Vertue* had some interesting experiences too. As mentioned in my account, June 13th, he lost his mast soon after leaving Plymouth. He started off with a small jib, but thought he would change to a big genoa to race the other boats and the extra press of sail snapped his mast in two. He put back to Plymouth and Mashford Bros., the five brothers who own a well-known boatyard in Plymouth, worked all the weekend to rebuild and re-rig the mast by Monday, two days later. David started again, and followed much the same route that I had, along the 50th parallel. He passed over Flemish Cap just east of the Grand Banks which I also passed over. Fifty miles south of Cape Breton he encountered a Canadian frigate which closed him on his weather side, drifted down on top of him and carried away one of his spreaders. After that he proceeded along the Nova Scotia coast in thick fog as I had and at one time he heard and then saw breakers ahead of him, tacked immediately but lost his log on the rocks in doing so. He proceeded along the same route as myself down to Cape Cod. In a Force 7 blow he sailed through Pollock's Rip just south of Cape Cod although he hadn't intended to. He went inside Martha's Vineyard and went aground for a while in Woods' Hole in the middle of the night, as a result of getting very tired with no rest for two nights. His main boom, swinging, hit him a crack on the head and fractured his skull; but David's fibre is tough and he battled on. He crossed the finishing-line 56 days after the start of the race.

My dreaded rival, the black-bearded Viking, went down past the Azores to the 36th parallel. He reached Bermuda on July 24th, 43 days out. From the Azores New York is only 500 miles farther than Bermuda. At his rate of progress he would have made New York in 50 days had he gone straight there and I believe he could have given Blondie a close race if he had not hauled into Bermuda. As it was, his time for the race was 63 days. His race was intensely interesting to me because I had nearly decided on the same route – the 'flying-fish route' as I called it in expectation of finding flying-fish on deck for breakfast at that latitude – instead of the ice-fog-headwind Great Circle. I gave the Great Circle route three votes and the flying-fish route two votes. After the start when I had been kept on a south-westerly course for three days by the strong headwinds and was off Ushant I very nearly continued on south-west to the flying-fish route. Today I wonder what would have been the result; I certainly do not know. (By the way, my wife and I kept close to this route on our sail home from New York and we did have flying-fish on the deck twice. Also a number of small squid.)

Jean Lacombe in *Cap Horn* arrived on August 24th. He seems to have followed the flying-fish route as far as the Azores but then instead of sailing along the 36th parallel he kept to the 39th. According to ship sightings, he placed himself in the middle of the strongest stream of the Gulf Stream about 1,000 miles east of New York and had only advanced 100 miles during 10 days. He would have to sail 4 hours a day, perhaps more, to make good the current of 1–4 knots against him before he made any progress towards his objective. I think that he cannot have had a copy of the U.S. hydrographic charts. These charts not only show the average of all the winds over many years, the iceberg limits, sea temperatures, fog possibilities, percentage of gales, hurricane tracks and magnetic variation but also the average tracks and speed of the Gulf Stream and North Atlantic currents for each month. Had he changed his position by 180 miles south or by 250 miles north-west he would have got out of the main Gulf Stream. Not only was he making the slowest passage but also had the smallest boat, so that he had the doubled disadvantage of taking longest and having least room for stores. Even on the Great Circle route we had about 0·4 knot current against us right across. That is to say about 9½ miles of adverse current to make good every day before starting to make any progress towards the destination.

When I got into New York I had to proceed to Staten Island. There to meet me was a captain of the U.S. Air Force and his mission was to find out if I had had any uncanny experiences or felt peculiar or if I had done anything odd during my 40 days of solitude. I couldn't think of anything but of course after being alone for that time one is naturally anxious to oblige. Psychiatrists seem to attach great importance to hearing voices. Yes, I suddenly remembered, I did hear voices once. This was off George's Bank in US waters and I was opening my last bottle of gin. Startled by voices I popped out into the cockpit and there were the owners – about five people sitting up on the top deck of a big steamer just going by, obviously enjoying their evening cocktails.

I need not have worried about being unable to think of any queer behaviour of mine because in the end he said that he was investigating the effects of solitude with a view to forecasting what it would be like for the astronauts when projected into space. I'm relating this because since then I've come to some conclusions about it. First that the sailing solitude doesn't have a real bearing on what the space travellers are likely to experience. On recalling some of my flights, I think that the sort of desolate loneliness you can experience in the air is quite a different matter. In 1931, nearly thirty years ago, I was making a solo flight in a seaplane from New Zealand to Japan, the first time that a long-distance flight had been made solo in a seaplane. I was crossing from New Zealand to Australia, 1,450 statute miles of a sea crossing and I was having a rough time between the small island of Lord Howe and the Australian continent. I had motor trouble, got into a severe small storm, and for hour after hour, had been expecting to be dumped into the sea. I remember that in this situation I had a desolate feeling of loneliness, such as I've never experienced at sea. When I reached safety and friendly people I felt cut off from them by a bottomless gulf of loneliness. I wrote then, 'If man ever flies alone out of the earth's atmosphere into space – to the moon – though he return safely, he will not live. The awful emptiness of space will change his soul and isolate it. Never again will he be able to make contact with man, beast, plant, or anything. And across the gulf of unutterable loneliness cutting him off from the world he once knew, he will only see distantly through a film of strange, hard air. Perhaps the soul, belonging to space, will have recognized its home, and languish in utter loneliness for it until, loosening its hold on the body, it floats back again.' This was my view nearly thirty years ago. Well, we shall soon know now. I wonder how it will turn out.

In this race I lost 10 pounds and I think I did a tremendous amount of work with my heavy gear. Blondie Hasler, who asserts that he did no work and held the helm for only one hour between the two continents also lost 10 pounds. David Lewis who had the most dehydrated foods and antibiotics, medicines and what not, lost 20 pounds. Val in *Eira* lost 18 pounds.

During my race I wrote a diary account of 50,500 words. You may wonder how I managed to do this when I complained continually of being overworked. Daily after breakfast when I had come through the night and was feeling rather pleased and optimistic with the next night some way off, I used to settle down, get out my blue book and imagine I was talking to my wife or some friend. I used to look forward to it. And again later in the day with a glass of whisky in hand.

If you ask me whether I would enter for another solo Atlantic race, I would answer that perhaps it is a bit too soon after this one to say, but I do feel I learned so much that I could knock time off my present record if I had the gear and boat that I would like and it certainly would be great sport to try.

SOLO ATLANTIC RACE 1960

Gipsy Moth III

SAIL CHANGES

	No. of times set	Total of hrs. set	Average No. hrs. set
No. 1 jib (genoa)	17	398·58	23·28
No. 2 jib	11	246·00	22·22
No. 3 jib	7	144·45	20·41
No. 4 jib	1	24·00	24·00
No jib set	3	12·50	04·17
Ghoster jib	3	22·05	07·22
Full mainsail	23	418·00	18·10
Main with one reef	6	42·50	07·08
Main with two reefs	4	37·35	09·24
Main with three reefs	6	58·04	14·21
Trysail	7	79·15	11·19
No mainsail or trysail	25	186·56	07·29
No. 1. jib boomed out as spinnaker	2	35·22	17·41
No. 2 do.	2	33·22	16·41
Bare poles	5	47·50	09·34

WIND

On the wind	636·24 hrs. = 26 days 12 hrs. 24 mins.
Wind-free	288·16 hrs. = 12 days 00 hrs. 16 mins.
Bare poles	47·50 hrs. = 1 day 23 hrs. 50 mins.
Total	972·30 hrs. = 40 days 12 hrs. 30 mins.

FOG

16 times   345·02 hrs. = 14 days 09 hrs. 02 mins.
This amounts to over 1,430 miles of the route.

BEAUFORT WIND SCALE

The wind speed on the deck of the yacht is probably 10% less than at 33 feet.

Beaufort Number	Wind speed in knots 33 ft. above sea-level	Wind Described	Sea Described
Force 0	Less than 1 knot	Calm	Sea like a mirror.
Force 1	1–3 knots	Light air	Ripples with the appearance of scales are formed but without foam crests.
Force 2	4–6 knots	Light breeze	Small wavelets, still short but more pronounced. Crests have a glassy appearance and do not break.
Force 3	7–10 knots	Gentle breeze	Large wavelets. Crests begin to break. Foam of glassy appearance. Perhaps scattered white horses.
Force 4	11–16 knots	Moderate breeze	Small waves, becoming longer; fairly frequent white horses.
Force 5	17–21 knots	Fresh breeze	Moderate waves, taking a more pronounced long form; many white horses are formed. (Chance of some spray.)
Force 6	22–27 knots	Strong breeze	Large waves begin to form; the white foam crests are more extensive everywhere. (Probably some spray.)
Force 7	28–33 knots	Near gale	Sea heaps up and white foam from breaking waves begins to be blown in streaks along the direction of the wind.
Force 8	30–40 knots (39–45 mph)	Gale	Moderately high waves of greater length; edges of crests begin to break into spindrift. The foam is being blown in well-marked streaks along the direction of the wind.
Force 9	41–47 knots	Strong gale	High waves. Dense streaks of foam along the direction of the wind. Crests of waves begin to topple, tumble and roll over. Spray may affect visibility.
Force 10	48–55 knots	Storm	Very high waves with long overhanging crests. The resulting foam in great patches is blown in dense white streaks along the direction of the wind. On the whole the surface of the sea takes a white appearance. The tumbling of the sea becomes heavy and sock-like. Visibility affected.
Force 11	56–63 knots	Violent storm	Exceptionally high waves. (Small and medium-sized ships might be for a time lost to view behind the waves.) The sea is completely covered with long white patches of foam lying along the direction of the wind. Everywhere the edges of the wave crests are blown into froth. Visibility affected.
Force 12	64–71 knots (73¾–81¾ mph)	Hurricane	The air is filled with foam and spray. Sea completely white with driving spray; visibility very seriously affected.

GLOSSARY

After-peak The lazarette or small hold under the counter.

Batten, sail A long thin strip of plastic or wood inserted in a pocket of the mainsail to keep the outer edge from curling or flapping.

Block Pulley.

Boom A wooden pole with one end attached to the mast – used to keep a sail outstretched.

Bowse down To pull down forcibly with a rope or tackle.

Brail To gather a sail together with a rope round it.

Burgee A triangular flag, usually of a club, hoisted to masthead; useful for showing the wind direction.

Check To slack away a rope gently while keeping a strain on it.

Cleat A two-horned piece of wood bolted to a yacht for securing the end of a rope.

Clew The corner of a sail at the foot and outboard (*see* sheets).

Counter The curved overhanging part of a yacht's stern.

Cringle An eye or hole in a sail, usually protected by a metal eyelet.

Dodger A length of canvas or terylene lashed to the life-line and bulwark to keep spray out of the cockpit.

Dolphin A large post or pole driven into the river bed for boats to be moored to the top.

Earing A length of cord attached to the sail to draw part of it to the boom when reefing.

Gaff A spar or pole with one end attached to a mast and the other end cocked up.

Genoa or genny On a yacht usually the biggest jib with a long foot reaching from the stem to well aft of the mast. *G.M. III's* genoa is the No. 1 jib of 380 square feet; the ghosting genoa, a light jib of 385½ square feet for zephyrs.

Gooseneck The fitting at the end of a boom for attaching the boom to the mast.

Goosewinged On a yacht it describes a jib set on the opposite side to the mainsail, usually poled or boomed outboard.

Grommet A ring of rope made up to appear endless. A deck quoit is a grommet.

189

Guy   A rope used to steady or keep in position anything which otherwise would move.

Gybe   Turning a yacht downwind from one side of the wind to the other.

Halliard   In a yacht it is a rope of wire or cordage used to haul the head of a sail up a mast.

Hank   A metal link for attaching a sail to a stay.

Jib   A foresail. Formerly a sail set or tacked to the jibboom or bowsprit projecting forward from the stem; now the name for any foresail set on the forestay from stem to mast. *G.M.* has 5 jibs from the ghosting genoa of 385 square feet to the storm jib of 65 square feet.

Jigger   For *G.M. III* a short length of rope which can be attached to a taut rope so as to take the strain off it. Useful to release a sheet jammed on a winch.

Jumper strut   Usually a short length of wood at right angles to the mast with a wire or jumper passing over the end of the strut to the mast, above and below, like a drawn bowstring and an arrow. It prevents the mast from bending.

Kedge   For a yacht a kedge means a light anchor usually on a rope; and kedging means using a small anchor to haul the yacht off mud or sandbanks.

Lee helm   Helm pushed over to the downwind side.

Leech   The sloping edge of a sail. It is the edge outboard or farthest aft.

Leeward   Downwind.

Log   A propeller drawn through the water, operating a mileometer on the yacht to register the distance sailed.

Luff   To head up the yacht towards the wind, also the leading edge of a sail.

Pay off   To slack away or fall off to leeward.

Pendant   A short length of rope, usually with a block or eye at the lower end.

Piston hanks   *See* Hank.

Port   Red – left-hand side looking ahead.

Preventer   A rope to limit the movement of something on a yacht, such as a boom. (In 1711 it meant an extra rope used for additional strength.)

Pulpit   A metal framework projecting forward from the stem or aft from the stern.

Purchase   A device for increasing an applied pull.

Putty   Slang for mudbank.

Reach Sailing with the wind more or less broadside on.

Reef To roll or brail up the lowest part of a sail to reduce the windage.

Reeve Thread or pass a rope through.

Rode Wind-rode means caused by the wind to head upwind; tide-rode means caused by the tide to point upstream.

Runner A rope with a tackle or purchase for staying a mast from aft. In a yacht the bottom end can be released from the deck.

Seize To bind together with cordage.

Sewed Grounded with the waterline above the water-level.

Shackle A link which is opened and closed to join chain to anchor, sheet to sail clew, etc.

Sheave Pulley-wheel.

Sheet The rope attached to the corner of a sail outboard or farthest aft.

Shroud A wire rope used to stay or hold a mast in position.

Slatting Flapping with a sharp crack.

Slide A piece of metal moving along a metal groove or track. The mainsail is attached to a number of these which slide up the track on the mast.

Sole Cabin sole means the floor of the cabin.

Spanker A fore-and-aft sail with boom and gaff at the aft end of the ship.

Spinnaker A sail ballooned out by poling a corner outward.

Spreader A small spar between the mast and a shroud.

Starboard Green – right-hand side looking ahead.

Stranded A rope with one of the strands parted or broken.

Strop A spliced ring of rope.

Tackle Blocks and rope used to increase a pull. A three-part tackle has three 'parts' of rope at the moving block and increases the pull by nearly three times.

Tiller-line A length of cord for holding the tiller in position or controlling it.

Topping lift A halliard or stay with a tackle for lifting a boom.

Transom The flat end of a yacht which gives the stern a sawn-off look.

Warp A rope such as used for moving a ship.

Weather, to Means towards the direction from which the wind is coming.

Whipping A binding at the end of a rope to prevent fraying.